THE ART OF MARKETING

The Art of Marketing

BY

Gerardo Escudero Samara
COPYRIGHT@2020

THE ART OF MARKETING

THE ART OF MARKETING

DISCLAIMER

The information in this book are provided for educational purposes only. The author and publisher shall have neither liability nor responsibility to anyone with respect to any loss or damage caused or alleged to be caused directly or indirectly by the information contained in this book.

THE ART OF MARKETING

TABLE OF CONTENT

Introduction
Marketing Overview
Sales And Marketing
The Marketing Environment
Buyer Behaviour
The Market Offering Of An Organisation
Marketing Target
Branding Strategy
Pricing Strategy
Strategy For Distribution
Communication And Relationships
Level Of Personalised Content
Marketing Management
Digital Vs Traditional Marketing
What Marketing Automation Means?
What Can Marketing Make You?
Why Sales And Marketing Must Align
Common Marketing Mistakes
Pillars Of Marketing Success
Why Is Digital Marketing So Important

COPYRIGHT

In no way is it legal to reproduce, duplicate, or transmit any part of this document in either electronic means or in printed format. Recording of this publication is strictly prohibited and any storage of this document is not allowed unless with written permission from the publisher. All rights reserved.

The information provided herein is stated to be truthful and consistent, in that any liability, in terms of inattention or otherwise, by any usage or abuse of any policies, processes, or directions contained within is the solitary and utter responsibility of the recipient reader. Under no circumstances will any legal responsibility or blame be held against the publisher for any reparation, damages, or monetary loss due to the information herein, either directly or indirectly.

Respective authors own all copyrights not held by the publisher. The information herein is offered for informational purposes solely, and is universal as so. The presentation of the information is without contract or any type of guarantee assurance.

The trademarks that are used are without any consent, and the publication of the trademark is without permission or backing by the trademark owner. All trademarks and brands within this book are for clarifying purposes

THE ART OF MARKETING

only and are the owned by the owners themselves, not affiliated with this document.

THE ART OF MARKETING

INTRODUCTION

Before you get to understand what marketing management is it is important to understand what marketing is first. In layman's language marketing is the act of nurturing customer relations, preferably those that are profitable to the organization or firm. In the business world it is important for you to know the various terminologies used and how to apply them. Marketing management can be described as the thinking part of it. It seeks to describe the various aspects of the customer. Marketing is not just about advertising and making sells, it is about getting the customer's satisfaction.

It is very hard to run an organization without all the skills of marketing and management. That's why most successful individuals go for an introduction to marketing management. It is a course that will provide you with all the statistical skills of organizing and solving organizations problems. Marketing management involves many channels and forms. There are various aspects that have to be looked at when managing the marketing strategies of a particular firm.

The first thing you need to consider is the potential of the company that is what the firm has to offer. This should not be viewed in terms of the products only but also the services it can provide. Where most business people get it all wrong is that they put all their efforts in the business and end up forgetting about the customers' needs. This does not help in marketing the company's products since it should be seen from a customer's point, how the product is benefiting the customer. You need to understand all your customers' needs and satisfactions. You expectations should be to meet the customers' needs. Having full understanding of the customers' needs and implementing strategies to meet their demands will build a good customer relationship.

During marketing your goal should not only to win more customers but also to maintain them. This is achieved after building a good customer relation. If you come up with good products and services then there is no doubt that you will be able to get more customers and also maintain old ones.

In marketing management you should have a defined marketing channel for example you can have cross channel marketing where two forms of marketing supporting each other. A good example is a website and a catalogue. You can also use multi channel marketing where different marketing channels support each other. For example prints and a radio station that both advertise your websites and your products.

If you are marketing your company through a website then there are certain things you need to understand about internet marketing. For internet marketing you should start

THE ART OF MARKETING

by having a good domain name, the next thing is optimizing your websites through the search engines for you to create traffic to your website.

Now that you have had an introduction to marketing management it is upon you to take these challenges and put them into action for you to realize desirable profits. As much as it may not be that easy but it is worth the challenge.

MARKETING OVERVIEW

Marketing: What is it?

So, marketing- what is it? Basically put, it is the process of meeting a customer's need for gain or trade, usually profit in the context of most business organisations. Of course, this is a basic definition, as it involved many steps and can vary from organisation to organisation, consumer to consumer, market to market, and so on.

The Marketing Cycle

The process of marketing revolves around a few different aspects that act as a continuous cycle: Firstly, there is a need, want or demand by consumers which, in turn, create a market. This market is evaluated for its potential, and an organisation creates a solution to it, in the form of a product. This product is designed with specific features that satisfy the market's re□uirements to a certain extent, creating a value. An exchange takes place, and then the process repeats.

Consumer Choice and Value

Marketing directly affects the way a consumer judges the value of a product and the level of customer satisfaction they receive.

THE ART OF MARKETING

Value

Just because an organisation creates a product to meet a market's need, doesn't mean it's the only one, nor is it the best or worst. All consumers judge the value of a product, both before and after the purchase. As stated above, marketing is based on an exchange or trade: this means that a consumer parts with something for the product in question. This 'parting' gives the consumer the ability to judge the value and the level of satisfaction they experience.

It's important to remember that the trade doesn't always solely involve money. Of course, the majority of products are paid for with money, however there are other costs, such as time, that also go into the transaction.

Customer value can be calculated, conceptually, by dividing total benefits by total costs.

Total benefits include all of the tangible, physical gains of a product (known as the functional benefits), as well as the emotional benefits that go with the purchase. For example, a new pair of jeans provide the functional benefit of clothing and comfort, and the emotional benefit of being fashionable and making the wearer feel good.

Total costs include the obvious monetary cost, but also costs of the consumer's time, energy and even emotion. If

THE ART OF MARKETING

a consumer is stressed about a purchase, this would be considered an emotional or mental cost.

Therefore, the benefits divided by the costs gives a consumer's value of the entire product purchasing experience. Of course, not all of these turn out positive. The consumer may want the product, but if they believe the monetary or time cost was too high, outweighing the benefits gained, they will value the product very low. Consumers often experience what is known as the 'turmoil of the purchase' which is the cost they experience in acquiring the product, whether that be frustration with Queues in a store, or not having the correct size, and so on. 'Buyer's remorse' is the emotional conflict that a customer experiences after the purchase where they start to analyse whether there was enough value to justify their purchase- a good marketing strategy is to always reassure the consumer and create enough value for them to never associate this feeling with your product.

A good example is the Harley Davidson motorcycle. There are many different alternatives of motorbikes on the market more powerful and cheaper, however the brand Harley Davidson still presents a lot of value to a certain group of avid motorcyclists, simply because the brand carries more weight than the simply functional benefit. The customer gains more value from the prestige and image that the brand represents.

Customer Satisfaction

How expectations are met dictate the level of customer satisfaction in relation to a product. If a product over-delivers in comparison to what a consumer expected, satisfaction will be very high. The opposite is true from a low level of satisfaction. Marketing aims to ensure that customer satisfaction is high to ensure that their product has a positive reputation in the market place, as the resulting repeat purchase of a happy customer as well as the positive word-of-mouth is very profitable.

The market place is forever increasing their expectations with the rapid evolution of technology, competitors and social media. Modern marketing is not just the creation and delivery of the right product: it's also about managing expectations. A product will never please everyone, and it's important to ensure the greatest satisfaction within reasonable confines.

Relationship Marketing

Managing value and customer satisfaction has created what is known as customer relationship marketing, sometimes shortened to CRM. This basically means that organisations view the consumer as the ultimate judge of their product, and therefore, creating a good relationship whilst satisfying their needs leads to customer loyalty: a goal, all good marketers strive for.

Retaining customers in a market is a key driver in organisational success. Losing customers results in less demand for a product, and significant financial loss. Often, an organisation will encourage feedback, especially complaints, as this means that they can evaluate the weaknesses in their offering and attempt to employ a recovery strategy to retain the customer. It has been shown that making a mistake and then correcting it, be that via an apology, a refund or sending free stock, etc., can greatly increase customer loyalty.

With the rise of social media, bad feedback can reach further than ever before. Employing a customer recovery strategy can result is avoiding significant losses associated.

The Evolution of Marketing

Basically, the modern practices and concepts of marketing and promotion began roughly in the 1960s to 1970s. From that time to now, the view on marketing has shifted and evolved.

The first philosophy was called the production concept which focused on mass production of products and selling them to a market as is. However, organisations started to discover that just one product didn't always fit the demands of a versatile group of consumers. This is how the product concept developed, and it saw focus on differentiating a product's features. Following this came the selling concept, which revolved around utilising promotion and a sales force to drive sales through communication with the market.

The next step diversified marketing further, which, funnily enough, was called the marketing concept. This involved conducting business through connecting far better with consumers, segmenting the marketing, investigating their individual needs and maximising consumer value and customer satisfaction by tailoring the product to match, setting an appropriate price, communicating effectively and ensuring delivery was convenient. Basically, it put the consumer first, and answered them with production, selling and product concepts, rather than the other way around. This was a very internally focused concept and was extremely effective, employed by most organisations even today.

There is one last stage. Whilst not all organisations do this, the benefits of an organisation that focuses on what's known as the societal concept are ☐uite high. This is basically taking the above marketing concept and adding a socially responsible aspect to it. The societal concept looks externally and not just internally within an organisation. For example, products can be environmentally friendly, contribute to charities, sponsor events and so on that benefit the larger community. It revolves around making profit by simultaneously satisfying consumers and acting in a way that benefits society. The positive repercussions of this can be very beneficial for an organisation as consumers seek more from them than just a good product.

The Marketing Mix

Here it comes- the obligatory 4 Ps of marketing. Considered by some to be slightly out dated, the four Ps are the real pillars of all marketing practices: Price, Product, Promotion and Place. Often, a fifth P, Positioning, is added to this marketing mix.

Price refers simply to the cost of the product. As already mentioned, this is monetary cost, as well as other costs such as time.

Product revolves around all attributes of the offering that are created by an organisation to satisfy their needs.

Promotion is about the communication techniques that educate and persuade customers to be interested in the product.

Place, also known as distribution, are the logistical practices employed in bringing the product to the consumer.

Positioning refers to the marketing techni☐ue of where your product sits in the market and how it is viewed by consumers. It's basically a product's reputation: is the product a low cost alternative, or an expensive luxury item with lots of prestige and so on.

When the product is an intangible service, there are three additional Marketing Ps that are added to the marketing mix: People, Process and Physical Evidence.

People refers to the human element of the service being carried out, such as relationships, personability, experience and expertise.

Process is exactly what it sounds like: the steps involved in carrying out the service to produce a gain for the customer.

Physical Evidence are the associated tangibles that the consumer will experience during the service that have an impact on how a consumer rates the service. For example, the way a lawyer dresses or the quality of the tools a builder uses.

The Wholistic Marketing Approach

Also spelled 'holistic', this approach suggests that a perfect marketing organisation unites the four key elements in one united operation: The marketing mix (the Marketing Ps, above), Customer Relationship Marketing (CRM), Internal employee satisfaction and the external Societal marketing concept, all discussed above.

THE ART OF MARKETING

By conducting organisational operations with these four elements, a business ensures that its main priorities ensure the greatest potential for success and profit.

How Does Marketing Do This?

The marketing function of an organisation lends itself heavily to how successful an organisation is. This is because the marketing function investigates the current position, and develops strategies, formulates tactics and executes actions that all produce the benefits an organisation strives for.

A marketing plan is a living document that outlines marketing's analysis and proposed efforts over a particular time frame in achieving organisational success. It involves the following elements.

Overview and Executive Summary
As the title suggests, the first section is a Quick snap-shot of the entire marketing plan that will follow this section.

Current Position
This section outlines everything to do with the organisations position as it stands currently, both internally and externally. It analyses the current market and its trends, current competitors, all external related environments as well the organisation's strengths, weaknesses, opportunities and threats.

Objectives
The range of goals are outlined here, which can include financial goals as well as marketing goals, such as greater share-of-voice, market share, reputation, etc.

Strategy
The proposed approach that will be taken in order to answer each objective.

Tactics/ Action Plan
Detailed explanations of executable steps of the strategy that will deliver results to achieve the objectives.

Projected Performance
Forecasted results of each deliverable

Control and Evaluation
This section details how the entire plan will be monitored

Marketing is one of an organisation's most essential resources! It's absolutely crucial you get it right from the beginning because Marketing really is the backbone of an organisation. Think about it: your Marketing plan determines an organisation's name, branding, tone, imagery, positioning, tactics, strategy, approach, customer target, communication method, product range, pricing, service offering, distribution network, and so on.

Read the above again- it sounds like Marketing really defines the entire business, doesn't it? That's because it does!

The biggest mistake any organisation can do is to "just start" without giving even a little bit of thought to Marketing. You don't want to start designing products without defining what your target market actually want first; this dates back to very early business principles from the 80ies. We're in the 2010s now and you won't survive! Nor do you want to create a selling kit to give to your team without considering the organisation's identity, messaging, tone or branding. Could you imagine how ad-hoc and sporadic your social media accounts will look to your customers without a cohesive message or plan behind it all? You'll end up looking like you're running a teenager's profile, as opposed to a professional business.

It's essential to map out your overall Marketing Plan from day one so that the organisation is streamlined, effective and efficient when operating, because there is nothing more destined to fail than an uncoordinated business.

The world is too small and your competitors, too many and too smart for you to not take the market place seriously. Don't leave your total Marketing, Content and Communications strategy up to chance, and more importantly, don't do it by piece-meal, as this will lead to a non-cohesive plan which, in-turn, will confuse your customers and waste your resources; something no business can afford to do.

Marketing is a beast worth taking the proper time and investment to nurture, as you'll reap the benefits very Quickly. Conversely, if you neglect or fail to give it the right attention, it can be devastating just as fast. Trust me, it's not something you want to find out from first-hand experience.

As a Marketing Consultant, something everyone of my clients say is: "I wish I had have done more with Marketing earlier on." The longer you leave it, the harder it becomes to reverse the damage and get fixed!

Don't underestimate the power of Marketing! And if you feel that you're out of your depth with the whole thing, it's worth the investment to hire a consultant to map it all out with you. You'll thank yourself and them very Quickly.

SALES AND MARKETING

"What is the Meaning of Sales & Marketing and Their Advantages?" and, I have to say, it does a pretty awesome job of breaking down the differences, responsibilities, and links between sales and marketing roles. Why revisit this now? Because it has never been more apparent that the relationship between sales and marketing is still just as misunderstood as ever, especially with advances in marketing technology.

Setting the Record Straight

Many in the business world, especially those who rely on sales and marketing for success, don't actually have a concrete grasp on exactly what sales and marketing are. Yes, the two are linked, but they are not one and the same. Sales departments rely on marketing; marketing departments and strategies exist to feed sales (notice I didn't say "make" sales). You wouldn't engage in marketing if you had nothing to sell, and your sales strategy would be much less informed and successful if not for your marketing efforts. Yes, many old-school salespeople (or go-getter small business entrepreneurs) are □uite capable of drumming up business on their own, and may even have some tried-and-true marketing tactics up their sleeve - but few have the time, skill, or technological resources to effectively capitalize on the true potential of their market.

THE ART OF MARKETING

A common mistake made by older, more established businesses is to assume that salespeople are skilled at marketing and that marketing people are skilled at making sales. In some cases this may be true, but certainly not across the board. While trying to conserve capital, many of these companies will attempt to combine their sales and marketing departments, essentially tasking their employees with two job descriptions, and that's usually a bad move. It's no accident that more recently established companies, tech giants, and organizations that employ a large number of millennials are killing it with their marketing efforts.

Breaking It Down

As the tenfold article explains, some of the key responsibilities of a sales team include:

- Follow Up
- Relationship Building
- Closing
- Retention

The mark of a great salesperson is the ability to cultivate a personal relationship. Many consumers who have stayed loyal to the same brand, dealership, or salon for years will say that they appreciate the personal attention they receive there. It is not a marketing employee's responsibility to follow up with a salesperson's existing customer once the lead has been handed off, nor is it their responsibility to convert a lead to a sale, "close the deal," or make sure the client remains a client for many years. Short of having an outstanding relationship with a skilled salesperson, product quality and excellent overall experience are the main things that will bolster client retention.

On the marketing side, primary efforts are:

- Awareness
- Engagement
- Conversion (from anonymous to known)
- Retention

It is not a salesperson's job to generate awareness or buzz about their brand, product or service. If they are expected to use their energy to make sales by nurturing leads and relationships, then how can they also be expected to have the time to do the leg-work up front that brings those leads to the table in the first place?

The marketing department creates awareness, builds engagement by creating information that will invite audience members to take action, and targets and tracks engagement by motivating audience members to provide contact information or initiate a free trial or consultation (converting them from a cold prospect to a known lead or potential buyer). It is important to note here that the retention function of a marketing department doesn't really overlap the retention efforts of a sales team.

On the sales side, client retention refers more to the salesperson's efforts to use the client relationship to continually check in with the client, attempt to engage them in further discussions about additional products or services they may be interested in, and seek referrals to the client's friends and family members. On the marketing side, however, retention refers to maintaining a higher level of consistent engagement (through targeted marketing based on buying preferences, interests and history) so that the customer relationship doesn't end at the initial purchase. Those email newsletters you receive after becoming a customer somewhere are not random - they have a purpose and are often tailored to things you've viewed or expressed interest in. A sales team simply doesn't have the insights, time, or often the resources to execute these types of strategic campaigns.

The Fine-Tuned Coexistence Of It All

The ideal sales and marketing relationship is a symbiotic one. Marketers and salespeople work together to determine what consumers need and how to deliver it. Sales and marketing should motivate, inspire and feed one other. They should collaborate and coexist. In the hierarchy of the business food chain, sales and marketing should not be seen as rivals or equals, but counterparts. One truly cannot exist without the other, but their skill sets are not the same - especially today, where advances in technology require the modern marketer to have a very specific, honed, and competitive set of skills that most sales people simply do not need to have.

For this reason many marketers are introverted, analytical, and deep-thinking individuals. Whether they're crunching numbers and analyzing data, compiling reports on trends and conversion rates, or writing awesome ads and creating beautiful websites and collateral material, they are required to intensely focus on what works, what doesn't, and adjust their creative efforts accordingly. Usually a marketing department will have creatives, analysts, and more tech-oriented people (who dive into the numbers and algorithms behind advanced marketing tools).

In contrast though, many salespeople are extroverts - they light up a room, they have excellent "people skills," can easily relate to others, and have the ability to pick up on social cues that might actually help them close a sale. Oftentimes salespeople have a broader focus, preferring to spend their days with appointments and meetings - activities that build relationships - rather than sitting behind a desk doing what a marketing department does best. For this reason, many salespeople have administrative assistants to help them with follow-up, paperwork, appointment setting, phone calls, proposals, and calendar management. This type of functional assistant role is less widespread in the marketing realm.

THE MARKETING ENVIRONMENT

Environments Around An Organisation

For marketing efforts to be successful, an understanding of the environments around an organisation is vital as they can have varying different impacts on an organisation- these can be negative, positive or a mixture of both. Environments can be classified as two types: the micro and macro environments.

The micro-environment are all of the influential parties directly around an organisation, and thus have a close and direct impact. These include the organisation itself, its suppliers, competitors, partner companies, intermediaries, the customers, and public (such as the media, consumer groups and so on).

The macro-environment are all of the influential, over-arching parties that, whilst aren't in direct contact with an organisation, have a larger impact due to their nature. These include the demographics or characteristics of the larger markets and society, economic forces, the natural environment, technological forces, political, legal and governmental forces as well as larger cultural impacts.

Competitive Forces Within a Market

Competition always have a direct impact on an organisation. The best way to analyse the competitive strength within an organisation is to look at five key aspects:

(1) The current industry competition, or segment rivalry between organisations
(2) How much power the suppliers have
(3) How much power the customers/buyers have
(4) The potential threat of new competitors entering the market
(5) The threat of substitute products

By judging the extent of these five forces, an organisation can determine how tough the competitive force is within a market.

Market Analysis

Marketing must always be able to gain an understanding of the current situation the organisation is in within a market. By doing so, a marketing strategy and action plan can be devised to correctly leverage strengths, minimise or remove weaknesses, capitalise on opportunities and be wary of threats.

One way to analysis the market is through a SWOT Analysis- Strengths, Weaknesses, Opportunities and Threats. The first two are internal to the organisation and can be a list of what the organisation does well and what it doesn't do well. The last two are external to the organisation and comprise of a list of potential events on the horizon that an organisation must be always aware of to ensure that it can perform to deal with such events.

Market Research

Naturally, gathering information and performing research within a market is a fantastic way to gain knowledge on a market. There are many different types of research goals, such as those based on discovering the level of customer satisfaction, potential innovations, product redesigns to better match customer demands, product testing, promotional research and so on.

However, before anything is actually conducted, it is vital that a strong Marketing Information System (MIS) is established. All research has a benefit and a cost, just like customer value. A good set of rules and systems that compose an MIS should weigh up the benefits and costs of conducting research and to what extent.

After assessing the need for information and research, the MIS must also devise a system and strategy for effective data collection, analysis and distribution of the results to the correct parties.

This works alongside the natural progression of the research cycle: first, the problem must be clearly defined. The more concrete this definition, the better the research will be as there is a clearer target to aim for. Second, a research plan is developed. Third, the research is implemented and lastly, the data is interpreted and made available in a report.

Primary and Secondary Research

Upon conducting the research, there are two types of classifications, both with their purpose, benefits and costs.

Primary Research is when a team conducts a completely new, very tailored and specific research plan that aims to directly address the defined problem at hand. Whilst expensive both in a monetary and resource/timing sense, it aims to be the most accurate and most detailed to the problem it is attempting to address as all actions and efforts are specifically designed solely for that one problem. Primary research usually comes after secondary research.

There are a few common approaches to primary data research, most commonly exploratory, which is observing

Secondary research refers to absolutely every piece of research ever conducted before by other parties or by those on different projects to the defined problem at hand. These include past research plans and projects, internet research, and so on. Whilst cheap, abundant and very accessible, it is data that has been collected by other parties which means it may not perfectly fit the current defined problem, there may be accuracy issues, it may be too old or even biased.

Regardless of research type, data must aim to be relevant, accurate, current and impartial to be of any practical use.

Collecting Data For a Research Project

There are many different ways to collect data, each with their own characteristics, channels and methods.

Firstly, the approach. You can focus on the observational approach, which revolves around exploratory research by watching behaviour. The second is the descriptive approach through surveys and questions, and the last is the experimentative approach, which is utilising groups to determine the cause-and-effect relationship, known as causal research.

Collecting information can include online questionnaires, personal interviews, telephone interviews and focus groups.

Choosing a sample for research is another key attribute that can greatly affect the research outcome. Questions like how many, who is to be surveyed and how is the sample chosen are all important questions.

Probability Sample (random)

A simple random sample is where all members of the population have a completely equal chance of selection at random. A stratified random sample is where a particular characteristic is chosen first (such as age or location), and then from that specific group, all members have an equal chance of random selection. Lastly, a cluster sample, the total population is divided into a subgroup clusters and the research is conducted on those only, rather than the whole population.

Non-probability Sample (non-random)

A convenience sample is where the population most accessible is chosen. A judgement sample is where the researcher decides who to choose based on their belief of which population members best represent their target. A quota sample is where specific numbers of the population are the goal of the research, rather than random representation.

Big Data

THE ART OF MARKETING

Big data refers to the phenomenon where, today, huge amounts of easily accessible, live data is available pretty much at our fingertips, allowing people to make educated decisions almost instantly. Big data has rapidly changed every market and industry, especially with the rise of social media and the internet.

BUYER BEHAVIOUR

The Buyer Decision Process

Conceptually, a buyer or consumer experiences and progresses through a series of steps in regards to the acquisition of a product to satisfy their needs. They are as follows:

(1) Problem recognition
(2) Information search
(3) Evaluation of alternatives
(4) Purchase decision
(5) Post-Purchase behaviour

The size, complexity and frequency of this process depends on the buyer themselves and the nature of the purchase. Things like the cost, risk and impact of the outcome all influence the nature of this process. For example, a buyer will go through more carefully when purchasing a house versus a candy bar.

Problem Recognition

Once a consumer's actual state and ideal state are not aligned, a consumer senses a problem that requires rectification. If their actual state remains the same, but their ideal state lifts, this is the recognition of an opportunity or want (such as a nicer car or house). If their ideal state remains the same but their actual state falls, this is the recognition of a need (such as hunger of thirst).

Different consumer segments are driven differently and have different ideal and actual states.

Information Search

After a consumer identifies their need or want, they go on the hunt for information. This can include internal (memory or experience) and external (the internet, commercials, media, reviews, customer service, family and friends) sources.

There is also the bias of plain information versus persuasive information. A consumer must be able to determine which kind of information to follow and trust.

At the information search, a buyer begins to weigh up total benefits over total costs to determine their own feelings about how certain products may satisfy their needs.

Brand awareness and preference also comes into play here. An evoked set is a list of brands that a consumer is preferential to and lean more towards. An inert set are the brands that a consumer are impartial to and an inept set are brands that a consumer will avoid for whatever reason.

A good marketing strategy would be to make genuine and useful information readily available for consumers in the method and channels their categories tend to use more often.

Evaluation of Alternatives

After information is collected, a consumer will determine if there are other options or substitutes for their needs so they can determine the optimal gain, given their situation. It varies from consumer to consumer as some are careful thinkers whilst others are more impulse buyers, and they may place different value on certain products and industries over others.

The current context of the need also has relevance at the alternatives seeking level. For example, a consumer weighs up different restaurants depending on if they are eating alone, going on a date, are looking to spurge, celebrate a birthday, and so on. The context of their need places a significant skew on their choices.

Once a consumer has their alternatives figured out, they will rank all options depending on all different attributes they deem important. A good marketing strategy at this point is to ensure that your product is easy to rank by highlighting all of the features and benefits in order to persuade buyers to rank your product higher as a more viable option.

Decision

This is the point where the consumer decides to act, and it is literally as simple as choosing the alternative that was at the top of their ranking list, offering them the highest utility. Whilst original purchase intentions and engrained preferences do play a part in information search and evaluation of alternatives steps, the actual outcome may be very different as a different, originally unforseen product offered the best utility.

A good marketing strategy at the decision point is to reduce the perceived risk for the consumer, so utility value is far more appealing.

Post-Purchase Behaviour

After the product is purchased and consumed to satisfy the original need or want, the consumer determines how satisfied or dissatisfied they are. Their expectations play a big role in this- did their choice meet, exceed or disappoint their expectations.

A consumer can experience cognitive dissonance, also known as buyer's remorse, at this stage. Due to the large amount of choice in a market place, internal conflicts can occur where the consumer becomes nervous, wondering if they had made the correct decision.

The best marketing strategy to employ here is, only promise what your product can deliver, reassure your customers that they've made the right decision and, if dissatisfaction occurs, encourage feedback and rectify the situation to turn them into satisfied customers again.

Influences on Consumer Behaviour

There are several influences that greatly impact on buyer behaviour, some more than others. From least to most:

(1) Culture and society
(2) Social (reference groups, family, friends, status)
(3) Personal (age, life cycle stage, economic situation, lifestyle, personality)
(4) Psychological (motivation, perception, leaving, beliefs and attitudes)

Culture and society are basically the groups and social norms that a buyer tends to gravitate to and associate with.

Social influences refer to parties externally close to the buyer, such as family and friends. It also refers to the role different parties play, whether or not the buyer is the user, the influencer, the initiator, etc. too.

Personal influences are the factors and attributes of the buyer themselves on a physical level, such as their ages, occupation, etc.

The psychological influences are on an internal, mental level and revolve around the way a consumer thinks. Therefore, their perception, approach to motivation, the way they learn and interpret stimuli, and their ingrained beliefs and attitudes.

Marketing is able to utilise and adapt to these influences in order to reach the target market, catering messages to them personally.

When the Buyer Is A Business: B2B Marketing

B2B Marketing is a buzz word for business to business marketing and trade. In other words, not a business to consumer situation. Business to business trading also fits into the buyer behaviour theory as a business still acts as a buyer on a basic level: it's just, due to their nature, it becomes slightly more complex. A common misconception is that B2B marketing is based more on facts than an emotional purchase, as is quite common for an individual buyer, but this isn't always the case. Whilst businesses have systems and procedures in place to enact purchasing, the people involved in the process are still people.

B2B Decision Process

Previously, the five main steps of an individual buyer's decision process was outlined. For a B2B buyer, the process gains a few extra steps simply due to the nature that purchases are privy to policies and approval systems.

(1) Problem recognition
(2) General need description
(3) Product specification
(4) Supplier search and short-listing
(5) Proposal solicitation
(6) Supplier evaluation and selection
(7) Order routine specification
(8) Performance review

Simply put, an organisation or business's needs are different to an individual's needs. When a business looks to purchase something, it is usually for the organisation to use in their main course of business, which is why the need has to be elaborately detailed and then suppliers are sought after to tender for the need fulfilment. Once this occurs and a supplier is found, routine purchases tend to occur until there is a review.

Questions To Ask To Understand A Buyer

There are a few ☐uestions that can be asked to assist in better understanding the target consumer and their buying process.

THE ART OF MARKETING

(1) What do they think and feel?
(2) What do they see in the environment?
(3) What do they hear from close influences?
(4) What do they say and do?
(5) What causes them pain and frustration?
(6) What causes them gain?

THE MARKET OFFERING OF AN ORGANISATION

A market offering is the scope of products that an organisation offers to customers. A product can be a tangible good, a performed service, an experience, an event, a place, information, innovative ideas, industries or even companies and people themselves (or a combination of a few).

Quite often, a product offering is a combination of a few. There are pure good, such as oil or computer components, and there are pure services such as surgery or investment advice. A combination can be based on Fast Moving Consumer Goods (FMCG), where, for example, bread is baked; luxury goods, such as wine or perfume where the bottle is a tangible good but there was a focus on the service of creating it; and even familiar services such as fast food, where the good is the food but the speed is a service.

Understanding the market is vital to all successful marketing strategies as it allows a tailored and efficient product portfolio.

Categories of Consumer Products

There are four types of products:

THE ART OF MARKETING

(1) Convenience products- which are frequently purchased items, usually immediately or on a whim, that require little buyer decision and effort, such as a candy bar or chewing gum.

(2) Shopping products- slightly more expensive and have a long life. A customer usually takes a moderate amount of time in research to find the best match for their needs, such as white goods or a car.

(3) Specialty products- customers make an extra-special effort for these products as they are not common or have unique qualities, and are therefore willing to spend more on buying efforts. For example, jewellery or antiques.

(4) Unsought products- these are products that the consumer either doesn't know about or a product that the consumer doesn't really intend purposely on purchasing, such as taxes, or donating blood.

Naturally, these can vary depending on the individual, but the classifications hold true. However, the motivation behind the purchase could be positive (excited to go out and buy) or negative (reluctantly buying due to a need).

Services

THE ART OF MARKETING

Services are an intangible product that are an action for the benefit of the buyer, but after competition, the buyer doesn't own anything. Services are a rapidly increasing area of the economy, with approximately 70% of Australia's Gross Domestic Product (GDP) comes from the service industry.

Services have the following characteristics:

(1) Intangibility

(2) Inseparability (the provider and service cannot be separated and therefore consumption must be planned at a convenient time for both parties. However technology has begun to overcome this).

(3) Variability (the service is performed, so it can be slightly different every time depending on the provider, when, where and how).

(4) Perishability (Services cannot be consumed at a later date)

(5) Related tangibles (a service usually involves related tangibles such as a builder's tools or the suit and office of a lawyer. Consumers will judge a service on the related tangibles.

Consequences of Service Characteristics

Services have a unique set of characteristics due to their nature.

>(1) Evaluation: it's hard to evaluate before and even after purchase

>(2) Exposure to a service before purchase can only be through word-of-mouth and related tangibles.

>(3) The product revolves around imperfect people: it's very hard to keep the service consistent every time.

>(4) Often, consumers are part of the service delivery (such as education), and they cannot be easily controlled or managed.

The Three Levels Of A Product

A product of any type has three levels.

>(1) The core customer value: what is the consumer actually buying? What is the final benefit they receive from the product?
>For example, with an airline, the core value may be time-critical transport.

>(2) The actual product: brand name, features, design, packaging, etc.

With the airline example, this would be the plane, the safety record, the seat allocation, the meals, and so on.

(3) The augmented product: the external and packaged benefits such as support, warranty, after-sale service, etc.
With the airline example, this is the frequent flyer schemes, tour packages, priority check-in, etc.

The Product Life Cycle

A product goes through several different stages in its overall life. The scope and time frame differs depending on the product and industry, but all products experience this inevitable cycle.

(1) Product development: losses and investment costs are high and sales are at zero, as the product is being designed, developed and tested.

(2) Introduction: the product is first released into the market. Sales are low but begin to climb with time as communication and education start to filter into the mark. Investment costs still may be high as tweaks are made and losses are usually still incurred here.

(3) Growth: the product is growing rapidly as the market begins to notice. Sales climb quickly and profits begin to be made.

(4) Maturity: Sales are at a peak high and start to plateau out as the market becomes saturated. The product is no longer new but is well known with a solid reputation. Many companies with a good product or brand will aim to initiate ways to keep it at this phase, such as most cola soft drinks.

(5) Decline: sales start to drop as the market demands new and better products to replace the current one, causing it to fall out of interest.

The Need For New

From the product life cycle, it is easy to see how it's very important for organisations to continually focus on refreshing their current product offering and continuing to innovate with new products in order to remain successful. An organisation cannot continue to only focus on one brand forever, especially if that product is in the later stages of the product life cycle.

Market changes, whatever they may be, cause an eventual decline for a product, whereas new products are fun and intriguing, as spur growth for an organisation. A new product can be:

(1) Entirely new to the world, creating a new market

(2) New for the organisation, entering into a new segment previously untouched by that organisation

(3) Additional lines to the current product, such as spin offs, new flavours, and supplement products

(4) Product improvements through new features and designs

(5) Repositioning the image and target customer of a current product, causing a whole new segment to gain interest in it

(6) Cost reductions- reducing the cost increases the appeal of a product

Unfortunately, it's always not as easy as just creating a new product. New also implies untested and entering into uncharted territory, meaning that things can go wrong and new products can fail. The main reasons why new products fail could be because:

(1) the organisation over-estimated the potential demand, and the small sales cannot sustain it

(2) a bad or poor product design

(3) The product is badly positioned, priced or communicated to the market causing backlash

(4) Research findings were incorrect, causing bad judgements to be made

(5) The costs of research and development become too high or cannot be justified

(6) Competitors create obstacles and barriers to entry

(7) The brand becomes 'stretched' too far, ruining its reputation with the market

New Product Adoption

When a new product is released, there are five major factors that contribute to the rate of how quickly the target market notices and views the product with value.

(1) Communicability- which is, how well it was advertised and promoted

(2) Relative advantage- what the product offers better than others currently in the market

(3) Compatibility- how much does the market have to change their behaviour to utilise the product

(4) Complexity- or ease of use

(5) Divisibility, or trialability- can the market give it a trial before committing to buy

New Product Development Stages

An organisation develops a new product in a series of stages. Due to the rapid product life cycles of current products and times, the whole new product development stages need to ☐uicker than ever. Some organisations like to wait for a worthy product to go through the entire set of stages, whereas others will engage in innovative churn (where they put almost every product through and see how the market responds) to gain an innovative image.

Each stage is pretty self-explanatory from its name:

(1) Idea generation

(2) Idea screening

(3) Concept development and testing

(4) Develop marketing strategy

(5) Business analysis

THE ART OF MARKETING

    (6) Product development

    (7) Test marketing

    (8) Commercialisation

In developing a new product, an organisation must consider the following attributes:

(1) The threshold attribute: these are the basic functions that a customer would expect first and foremost when looking at the product to satisfy a need. For example, a dishwasher is expected to clean dishes.

(2) The performance attribute: these are the features that add a little more satisfaction to the product offering, above the threshold expectation. For example, a dishwasher with specifically programed cycles and times to save time and money. Or an internal rack that can change shape to fit different dishes.

(3) The excitement attribute: these are the 'wow' factor features, well above the previous two attributes that really impress the customer way beyond their expectations. Innovative products lie here as the offer features never seen before that, presumably, really meet the customer's needs. For example, the dishwasher that, for some technological breakthrough, never needs washing powder and still delivers clean dishes every time.

THE ART OF MARKETING

As always, these attributes can differ by consumer groups, product type and industry, not to mention that the excitement attributes downgrade to performance and finally threshold attributes as time and technology move onward.

A strong marketing strategy is to invest in improving performance or wow factors rather than improve the threshold attributes.

MARKETING TARGET

An organisation's best strategy when deciding on the product offering is to segment the market into a group that will be called the target market. A mass market approach is simply too difficult and wasteful, whereas it is far more effective or efficient to focus all energies into a particular group with similar characteristics and needs. By doing so, an organisation can cater their business model to service this market and gain the most return.

Through target marketing, an organisation can offer a tailored effort to meet the specific demands of a small segment, and in doing so, satisfy customers without spreading resources too thin.

A segment can be divided by geography, demographics, psychographic/lifestyle and behavioural factors. Modern marketing focuses more on behavioural segmenting rather than geography. There are additional segments when it comes to B2B segmenting, dividing with operating variables (such as technology), purchasing behaviour, situational factors, size of operation, industry and organisational characteristics.

There are three major steps in target marketing:

(1) Segmentation: this is where the market is divided into partitions based on key characteristics and

elements that are important to the organisation, such as age.

(2) Targeting: each partition is analysed based on how attractive, profitable and accessible they are and one or a combination are selected as the target market.

(3) Differentiation and Positioning: the organisation forms and executes a communication plan to advertise and promote the unique features and benefits of their product to the target market.

An organisation can segment based on however they see fit, however an effective segment has the following characteristics:

(1) Measureable: easy to ⬜uantify for research and results

(2) Substantial: enough to provide profits and sufficient opportunities

(3) Accessible: low in obstacles to reach

(4) Differentiable: distinguishable enough from other segments

(5) Actionable: strategies are able to be formulated to take advantage of the segment correctly

(6) Predictable: their behaviour is not sporadic or unmanageable.

Choosing A Segment

Analysing segments to select one can be done in two main ways:

(1) Top-down, which is start with the organisation and its capabilities and working out how to make the segment match.

(2) Bottom-up is analysing the segment and fitting the organisation to the segment.

Basically put, if a segment is highly attractive and the organisation has the strength to enter it, then it is a good segment. However if the segment looks poor and the organisation is not capable, avoid at all costs. The areas in the middle are □uestionable.

Product Positioning

In a segment, an organisation must position their product to how they want their consumers to view it. However, ultimately, it is up to the customers to decide their feelings toward the brand based on all experienced stimuli from the market.

A good marketing strategy will ensure the positioning is favourable and profitable for the organisation, as customers view the product as desirable based on their characteristics.

Changing a position is risky and tricky as positioning can become well ingrained. It could ruin or improve a product or brand's image. This is one some brands use a 'flank' strategy, creating a sub or related brand in the same market with a different positioning, such as Toyota and Lexus in the car market.

To choose a positioning strategy, an organisation must identify the competitive advantages their product and organisation, select the most desirable attribute from the viewpoint of the customers and then communicate this effectively with the target market.

Competitive Advantage

A competitive advantage is a feature, attribute, brand or other factor that gives one product offering something more favourable than all of its competitors in the market. This can be through product differentiation (eg: greater performance, or design), service differentiation (eg: better training or delivery), image differentiation (more desirable branding or events) or personnel differentiation (superior skills and training).

THE ART OF MARKETING

The correct competitive advantages must be chosen to create a unique selling proposition tailored for your target market. The criteria for deciding which differences to promote depend on how important, communicable, superior, distinctive, profitable, affordable and pre-emptive these differences are to the target market.

BRANDING STRATEGY

Branding is a large part of marketing as it encompasses so many things. A brand is a name, term, symbol, design or a combination of these used by an organisation to identify it as unique from others. It acts as an identity and signal, communicating many messages to the market. Position comes from the way the market views and connects with a brand. The strength of this bond and the value that customers place on a brand is known as brand equity.

A brand/label name is the part of a brand than can be spoken or written, made up of words, letters and/or numbers. Brand elements are all of the central components that make up a brand, such as the name, design, slogan, and so on.

Secondary associations in regards to a label are all the related elements, such as celebrity endorsements and product reviews.

A trademark, commonly associated with a label, is the legal registration and recognition of an entire brand by an organisation that prevents the incorrect or unauthorised replication or utilisation of it. A service mark is the same as a trademark, however specifically refers to a service offering.

Brand Equity

As mentioned above, the value customers place in a brand is known as a measure of brand equity. This value grows in stages:

> (1) Salience: this is general awareness of a label by the market, and is part of a general identity. The marketing strategy at this level is focused on determining who the brand is.
>
> (2) Imagery and performance are the visual association and product behaviour of a brand that communicate the features of what a label is to the market. At this level, the marketing strategy is focused on the meaning of the brand and what it is.
>
> (3) Feelings and judgements refer to the critical analysis and emotional connections that label has with the market, which communicate the personality of the label. At this point, marketing strategy is focused on response and what it is about the label that customers find appealing.
>
> (4) The pinnacle of brand equity is known as brand resonance. At this point, the label has a relationship with the customer and spurs a certain behaviour in

response to the label. Marketing strategy here is about fostering brand loyalty by focusing on what the label is worth to a customer.

Brand Development

There are two main approaches to developing a brand. An organisation can utilise a high budget and spend a lot of money to heavily communicate messages and increase awareness, or approach with a low budget, and instead, rely on other communication, such as word-of-mouth and very obvious brand names.

Depending on the approach above, the brand name can line on a spectrum from:

(1) Fictitious- such as Sony or Apple. The name is so obscure that it requires specifically teaching the market about what the product behind the label is or does.

(2) Associative- names that allude slightly to their product's function, but are conjured up on top.

(3) Suggestive- label names that are semi-descriptive but a slight play on words.

(4) Descriptive- such as Quick Copy or Pizza Hut. These names are more obvious

Obviously, the more fictitious end of the spectrum has the advantage of being unique and therefore easier to legally protect, however an organisation much teach the market about themselves (which may not always be a negative).

The descriptive side offers a far more descriptive and obvious name that signal the right kind of image when a customer hears it, however because they are so run-of-the-mill, it can be difficult to be unique and tricky to legally protect.

The goal of brand development is to increase brand equity so that the market pays attention and values a brand enough to generate popularity and sales. A good brand is strong, favourable, compatible with the product, unique and memorable.

Logos

A logo is the visual brand element or a brand, and can either be used with or without the name, depending on the knowledge of the target market. Logos can enhance or hinder and image, which is why it's important for an organisation to ensure it matches the brand well.

Label Association

There are several other brand elements that partner with a brand and impact on brand image and brand equity. These can be secondary associations, and include:

(1) The organisation itself and its branding (such as Nestle's Purina pet care sub-brand)
(2) The country of origin and its connotations (such as Italian wine or Swiss watches)
(3) Distribution channels (sold in nice stores, or particular outlets)
(4) Co-branding with other brands
(5) Characters (licencing and mascots)
(6) Celebrity endorsements
(7) Events and sponsorship associations
(8) Third-party sources (such as awards and product reviews)
(9) An associated slogan or jingle (to add more information or increase recall).

All of these elements impact on how the market values and sees a brand.

Brand Extension

Once a brand is in a market, an organisation may choose to extend its use. There are four types of brand extension methods.

(1) Line Extension: where the product category and brand is already in existence (such as adding flavours or colours)

(2) Brand Extension: New category, but an existing brand

(3) Multibranding: Existing category but new brand (Toyota and Lexus cars)

(4) New Brand: New product category and brand name

PRICING STRATEGY

Pricing and customer value are closely linked. Basically stated, the value a customer places in a product and brand is indicated by how much they are willing to give up, usually in the form of money. The price is the monetary value set by an organisation at a level they believe is worthy of their offering. However, if a customer wants a product, but the price is too high, their value analysis of the trade is lower than the price set and they won't make a trade.

This 'trade' for a customer, which is the price set from the perspective of the organisation, comes in many forms, such as rent, tuition, fees, fares, tolls, premiums, commissions, incentives and even bribes. Price is the only element of the marketing mix that produces an income for an organisation in the form of revenue. It is the one part of the marketing mix that is the easiest to adjust quickly, which is as to why organisations often opt to that element to spur a customer response to their offering, over changing the product itself, its promotion, people or distribution methods.

Bribes may be illegal in certain countries and acceptable in others, however in the illegal countries, it may be classed as other things, such as perks and added bonuses.

Who Sets the Price?

It is a typical accounting argument, where an accounting department of an organisation may believe it is their responsibility given that pricing involves monetary terms. This would be all well-and-good if the price was a simple recuperation of costs for the organisation. However, it is not that simple: pricing of a product speaks volumes to consumers.

This is why the task of setting price is with the marketing department: as the consumer receives a whole lot of messaging from the setting of the price alone. It signals to a customer what positioning and image the brand and product has. If it is expensive, often consumers will use it as a surrogate indicator for a judge of ☐uality. This is most common in the wine industry, where higher priced wines are often thought of immediately as better in consumption.

Therefore, marketing manage the price setting tasks as it indicates much more than simply cost plus profit. It isn't a simple e☐uation- it takes the department familiar with communicating with the target audience, as price is just another communication stream.

Price and Demand

THE ART OF MARKETING

As can be expected, the price of a particular product directly impacts on the amount of demand it receives from customers. The actual relationship is known as the economic term of price elasticity. Whilst in reality, nothing works as simply as economic models suggest, in general, a product with a high price elasticity of demand means that a change in price results in a large, corresponding change in ☐uantity purchased. Luxury and nonessential products tend to be within this category, as a large price increase will greatly drop demand, and visa-versa.

A low price elasticity of demand means that a change in price will not greatly affect demand shifts- this is known as inelastic demand. Less substitutable products and essentials full into these categories as, within reason, when price shifts, consumers still require them.

A more realistic approach to price and demand prediction is more toward the idea of pricing points. For example, if the price is high and ☐uantity is purchased for a luxury brand, and the price is suddenly dropped, initially, the demand would increase as consumers believe there is more value. However dropping the price further may then decrease demand, as consumers start to feel that the luxury brand is losing its exclusivity. This makes demand fall.

All of these types of factors must be taken into account by the marketing department when setting price of their products.

The Pricing Phenomena

As much as economic theory attempts to assume that consumers are rational, they just aren't when it comes to purchasing. The perceptions of value and price given by an individual consumer is so unpredictable that it takes the function of marketing research to really delve into why consumers think and act as they do.

Take, for example, bridal products. Large organisations over charge for pretty much everything to do with 'the big day', however the consumer is more than willing to pay as it's more of an emotional purchase rather than a rational, 'utility maximisation' purchase. A bride doesn't want a cheaper product, even if it is the same as an expensive version, as they value feeling expensive and exclusive and therefore justify the high prices.

Pricing as an Information Cue

As discussed before, price can be used as a surrogate indicator of quality, even if it's not true. In the customers mind, higher price raises expectations as the amount they have to trade for it is high. There are two associated pricing techniques relevant to pricing as a communicative device:

> (1) Price Skimming- this refers to setting the price very high, thus skimming the very top of the market's

customers. This creates an aura of prestige and/or technologically advanced status and is a good way to recuperate research and development costs, control initial demand and supply and generate high profit. However the product must justify this image if this technique is used.

(2) Price Penetration- this is when a product's price is set very low to attract high quantities of sales and obtain large uptake in the market before a competitor.

(3) Yield Pricing- setting the pricing to manage exact ☐uantities of purchasing. For example, if stock is perishable, the price may be discounted to increase numbers and then when supply is short, the price rises to manage this.

(4) Volume Pricing- setting a price to ensure high sale/bulk volume purchasing over profit per unit.

(5) Loss Leader- Pricing at a loss per unit to encourage impulse, related purchasing of other products in the same offering.

Pricing strategy all depends on the organisation's justification and rationalisation of all aspects of their marketing strategy.

Pricing and the Psychology Of Consumption

There is a directly psychological relation between pricing/cost and the consumption rationale of a consumer. Most organisations do not draw attention to the price as it represents a cost to the consumer, and they would much rather the consumer benefit from the product's value rather than them dwelling on how much they paid for it. This makes sense. This is why some organisations offer upfront bulk payments, season passes, bundling and so on.

However, as mentioned previously, consumers aren't always rationale and sometimes, the constant reminder of cost is motivating for them. Basically, a consumer who doesn't utilise their purchase will actively make a decision to not rebuy it. This means that charging upfront could make the consumer forget about the product (e.g.: a gym membership), and once they forget, they will not justify a repurchase, however smaller costs more regularly are more manageable in a consumer's mind and the constant reminder stimulates motivation for consumption, and therefore repeat purchase.

It all depends on the organisation's product offering and pricing strategy as to what approach they take.

Internal Pricing Factors: Objective Based

There are different types of objectives of consideration when setting a price, aiming to achieve a particular goal.

(1) Financial
These are strictly about monetary goals, such as setting price to achieve a gross profit margin of 23%, or Return On Investment (ROI) by 12% this year.

(2) Marketing
These revolve around market and consumer focused goals, such as increasing market share, gaining more consumer awareness or increasing brand loyalty.

(3) Societal
Pricing is set by the organisation based on managing a societal rationale. For example, adding into the cost a donation to charity, or carbon offsetting.

Internal Pricing Factors: The Marketing Mix

Does the marketing plan and current marketing mix support the proposed price? In other words, is the price set consistent with the expectations a consumer would have given the rest of the product's attributes. The price must be reasonably consistent and in context with the product's design, process, distribution, people, reputation, brand and positioning.

Internal Pricing Factors: The Market Classification

THE ART OF MARKETING

Pricing is also very subject to the type of market the product exists in. In a monopoly, there is only one offering organisation, so excusing government regulation, pricing can be set at whatever they wish. In an oligopoly, where there are a two to five large main players in the market, the strategy tends to be a lead and follow pricing strategy, basing price off the movements of the main competitors.

In a perfect competition market, where the product is an identical commodity, the price solely depends on the supply and demand of the time.

In a monopolistic competitive market, which is the typically normal market where many organisations are within a market offering substitutable yet differentiated products, pricing is set based more on each organisation's marketing plan.

Internal Pricing Factors: Organisational Considerations

Naturally, the management within an organisation decides who best to set the prices of all the elements within the product offering- this is known as the pricing process. Typically, in smaller organisations, price is usually set by management but in larger organisations, it is set by product managers within the marketing team. The most important part is that the person or people that set the price must have well informed insights into the customer and their perception of value.

Revisiting the Concept of Customer Value

Remember that customer value is total benefits over the total costs. Costs include a lot of pricing, such as the initial purchase price, maintenance and repair costs, ongoing fees, installation, training, financing and so on.

The benefits of the product, such as performance, features and Quality must outweigh all of the prices and costs to be worth the value to the customer.

Approaches to Pricing

There are three main approaches to setting a price.

> (1) Cost-Based
> Basing the pricing barriers (such as the price floor- the lowest possible price), on how much the product costs to produce. Generally, if fixed costs are Quite high, a part of the price is set lower to maximise volume sold. If variable costs are high, price can be set to maximise the per unit margin.
>
> The issue, again, is that this pricing is based on internal measures, rather than on the target market, and could communicate the incorrect message to

them. Still, the cost-based approach can be a background consideration.

(2) Competition-Based
As the name suggests, this is basing it on however the competition prices and differentiating a product based on their pricing strategy. However this assumes that the competitor has a good grasp on the target market.

(3) Value-Based
This approach bases costs on what level of value the target market places on the product itself. Then, the organisation can employ a price skimming strategy (pricing at the top value), price penetration (pricing at the lowest value) or somewhere in between. This requires a bit of research to discover what attributes and expectations the customer values the most and pricing it on this.

In reality, there should be a blend of the approaches. The price ceiling (or the price point at which demand becomes zero) should be set at the top, and the price floor (or the price point at which profit becomes zero) should be established first. The Price ceiling represents customer perception of value and the price floor represents the consideration for product cost.

The price is then set in the middle, in between these points, with all factors such as marketing strategy, objectives, competitors and market place factors taken into consideration here to find the ideal price.

The Value Based Approach

Basing pricing strategy on the target market is an obvious choice, given the impact price has in communicating with the target market. Through starting with the customer's value and working backward, a price can be settled on that will allow an organisation to best maximise the price per segment and manage customer value perceptions.

The Gift Economy

With technology increasing so rapidly, a 'gift-economy' also referred to often as a 'free-love' economy has emerged. This is where an organisation offers their main product as free and finds another solid revenue stream to gain profit from. Search engines are a good example of this, where the search function is free, but the Google adword service and other advertisements and services are paid for.

The issue with this is the consumers lose the perception of value when products, such as music and news) are available for free, online. This shift in mind-set is a rapid game changer for a lot of organisations as consumers start to question why they are paying for specific products. For example, years ago, customers would purchase a newspaper, because they saw the value as worth the money, however today, when news is so rapidly available online, they can no longer justify paying for it.

Today, organisations are creating business models where the consumer doesn't pay and then charges associated organisations for their access to these customers, such as YouTube or social media advertising.

This has the risk of becoming so extreme that it may get to a point where organisations will pay or reward the customer to use their product, rather the other way around, just to give them access to the customer to sell this onto other organisations for profit.

However, there is a predicted limit with this as over-exposure to secondary ads and the other revenue-gaining 'add-ons' will render them ineffective and these secondary organisations will avoid these business models.

The Freemium

This relates to the new pricing technique known as 'freemium'. A freemium is when an organisation gives the basic level product to the consumer for free and then charges for the premium use of it. This is very evident in free phone apps on smart phones, where the basic app is free to download and use, however the customer must pay to get the ad-free version or open up all of the service for them to use.

The Bait-and-Hook

A pricing technique where the main product is free or extremely discounted, however then the customer must purchase an expensive associated product to utilise the main product. An example of this is office printers, where the printer is given for free, and the customer has to purchase the paper and print ink off the printer's organisation.

STRATEGY FOR DISTRIBUTION

Distribution is the fourth element in the marketing mix, dubbed as 'Place'. Basically, it is everything involved with making the product offering available to the market. An organisation is faced with many options to get the product within reach of the consumer and that can be either through a channel or direct to market. Having distributors makes economic sense in certain contexts, however the organisation needs to trust the channel by giving up a lot of control.

Today, distribution channels are getting shorter and shorter with technology, which has been called 'disintermediation'. This basically means it is becoming easier to 'cut out the middle man to increase profits, maintain greater control and give the organisation direct contact with the customer.

The Strategic Value of Channels

In a more general sense, an organisation can usually cover the information, promotion, contact, matching and negotiation activities of a transaction, however the physical distribution can often be outside the scope and therefore outsourced by the organisation, especially when in the form of a physical good.

Intermediaries specialise in the essential distribution duties and can also offer value-add services like storage and warranty support, so often, it makes strategic and financial sense for, for example, a manufacturing organisation to enlist the partnership of such intermediaries to complete the channel flow, so they can focus on what they do more effective and efficiently.

The issue is, intermediaries are starting to gain a lot of power given that the other organisation relies so heavily upon them to make any sales at all. They can make all kinds of demands and then threaten to stop supplying the market the organisation's product should they not comply.

This is why some organisations attempt to shift the power using VMS, Vertical Marketing Systems.

Vertical Marketing Systems (VMS)

A VMS is where one part of the channel either purchases or sets-up their own distribution channel or intermediary in order to by-pass powerful distributors and do it themselves. The obvious advantage is that power goes to the original organisation and they have far greater control over the whole channel, even if they use their own and use another distributor, as diluting the stage means that the powerful intermediaries lose their monopolistic power.

The problem with a VMS is that it can be risky and costly to do as the organisation needs to learn to be a good distributor and retailer as well as a manufacturer. There is little use in setting up a VMS if the newly opened intermediaries do not have the right contacts or skill set to really compete with a specialised one.

Apart from a straight VMS, there are two other slightly different VMS models. The first is a contractual VMS, where another intermediary is not technically owned, however they are contractually secured by the other organisation, such as what is done in franchising. The other is a weaker administrative VMS, where an intermediary is not technically owned or contracted to the other organisation, however both organisations work together as partners.

The Intermediary Focus

Whilst this topic can become focused on the manufacturer as the only central focus of a distribution channel, the intermediaries are large players in the channel themselves. There are several intermediaries that have become very successful simply by finding manufacturers in a localised area and simply brought them together in one unified distribution model, creating a symbiotic relationship. An example is a meal delivery service, where the service promotes all of the food and the delivery to the customer, the customer orders through them, and then the meal delivery service places orders with local restaurants and delivers the food.

Influences on Channel Strategy

The strategy an organisation chooses is impacted by both external and internal factors. Internal factors include the organisation's strategy, goals, objectives, resources, skillset, control and marketing mix. External factors include customers, the market environment, competitors and intermediaries.

As is normal from a marketing focus, the key is to keep customers as a focus for all activities. Therefore, considerations such as what benefits they're seeking, what channels will provide the best access, which distribution strategy will position the product as the most appealing to them, and so on.

Online Shopping

This is a very popular trend in modern distribution strategy and is extremely popular with consumers. There are a few factors to impact on this type of distribution:

(1) Political
- Certain taxes can be avoided
- Legislation and consumer protection
- Loss of physical store jobs
- Government focusing on internet legislation and internet services (such as the NBN)

(2) Economical

- Globalisation of economies and markets
- Increased competition as physical restrictions are removed
- Currency exchange rates
- More informed, price conscious consumers
- Access to foreign products
- Cost advantages due to competitive pricing

(3) Social
- Social media has become a norm in society
- Other demographics are becoming more involved
- Socially acceptable to be thrifty
- Time poor customers have a need for convenience
- More accepting and tech savvy demographics
- Self-image is important, so customers can easily share their purchases online

(4) Technological
- Easier for all organisations to use and take advantage of
- Increase in accessibility
- Increased security on technology which increases buyer confidence
- More devices to access online shopping
- Big Data allows customers to be better catered to
- More advanced software to assist all stakeholders

(5) Environmental

- The shortening of the supply chain could reduce environmental impact
- Less need for bricks and mortar stores
- Customers are more environmentally aware
- Less physical distance, reducing barriers to access

Channel Levels

There are three main classifications of channel densities.

(1) Zero Level: where the manufacturer goes straight to the consumer direct, such as Dell computers.

(2) One level: where there is only one intermediary in between the manufacturer and customer, such as book sellers and Amazon.

(3) Multilevel: where there are many intermediaries, such as wholesalers and retailers between the manufacturer and consumers. In a multilevel channel, the producer can sell in one straight line (i.e.: one wholesaler and then on to one retailer, then the customer) or through many different intermediaries in different industries (such as agents).

Distribution Intensity

Distribution intensity refers to all strategies an organisation has for getting product through the channel.

THE ART OF MARKETING

(1) Intensive distribution
Where an organisation sends their product through a large variety of intermediaries, channels and stores for maximum access to the market. This type is mainly for simple, inexpensive and easily transportable products that tend to be repeat or impulse buys, given the consumer as much exposure and therefore opportunity for purchase as possible.

Typically, products that are intensively distributed are heavily promoted with low cost and high turn-over. The quality can also be average or low in general.

(2) Selective distribution
Where the organisation is slightly more selective about which channels they chose so as to not cut off all access to customers, but be more selective to give the product a different positioning to a commodity product. This is for products, such as specialty retailers and branded stores, that are more on the specialty or higher end, and therefore restrict certain levels of access to create an aura of □uality or provide more intimate customer service.

(3) Exclusive distribution
Where an organisation has a very low number of channels and outlets. This is a very restricted distribution strategy for very high-end, high

involvement products and give the perception of exclusivity and uniqueness.

Typically, products that are selectively or exclusively distributed are promoted exclusively, are priced high and the consumer will specifically seek the product as the quality and value is high.

All three distribution types position the product differently in the eyes of the consumer, hence why the channel strategy selected must be consistent with the marketing plan. Obviously this varies with product and industry type.

There are also two types of alternative strategies to the above to increase the flow of the distribution channel:

> (1) Pull strategy: the organisation advertises and conducts marketing efforts directly to the end consumer at the end of the channel, which increases their demand, 'pulling' products through the channel. To do this, the distribution must be so there is enough access provided for consumers to get the maximum effect.
>
> Such marketing efforts, besides straight promotion, could include free samples, trials, coupons, financing, discounts, specials and so on. Usually, these are quite successful as, being normal fast moving consumer

goods (FMCG), a consumer will tend to take advantage of these types of bargains.

(2) Push strategy: when the organisation advertises and conducts marketing efforts directly at other intermediaries within the channel to encourage their demand, 'pushing' products through the channel.

Marketing efforts in a push strategy involve incentivising intermediaries so as to encourage their demand, such as benefits to their sales forces, bulk discounts, financing and negotiation on marketing efforts to the end consumer.

COMMUNICATION AND RELATIONSHIPS

Promotion and advertising is the cornerstone of the marketing plan and marketing department, requiring a strategic plan to work out the best way to leverage marketing efforts to successfully promote a product.

The Promotion Mix

The promotion mix consists of advertising, personally selling, sales promotion, public relations and direct marketing, utilising the main elements of the original marketing mix. It depends on the product, industry and market as to which of the promotions mix to use, however usually a combination of two or more is the most effective way of communicating and sparking the interest of the target market.

Common trends have blurred the lines between which promotion method works well, and consumers today require very tailored messaging for them to actually pay attention to the marketing activity itself. "Same old" advertising is starting to get lost in the clutter, to be replaced by innovative and viral campaigns that engage consumers.

The IMC Approach

Integrated Marketing Communications (IMC) is the approach where all marketing efforts utilised by the organisation from the promotion mix communicate a clear, consistent and compelling message about the product or organisation themselves. Shifts in communication and message should be done slowly overtime, rather than confusing the customers by promoting inconsistent messages. IMC is a way that an organisation manages its entire portfolio of communication.

The Whole Communication Offering

An organisation is constantly communicating messages to the target market. These include:

(1) Planned and deliberate messaging: via the promotion mix

(2) Product messaging: via the marketing mix (such as price, distribution, etc)

(3) Service messaging: via interaction with the customers themselves

(4) Unplanned and uncontrollable messaging: via gossip, external publicity, reviews, rumours and other external environment buzz.

An IMC plan will ensure that an organisation presents a united, solid communication front to customers: this means the management of all contact points of an organisation and product (what is said in the promotional mix, confirmed by the unplanned messages, and performed via the product and service messages).

Elements in the Communication Process

All messages follow a process:

(1) The sender creates the message and encodes. By encoding, this means the process of creativity of the message.

(2) The message is then send out via the medium chosen. At this point is must also compete in amongst what is known as 'noise'- these are all of the conflicting messages and all other interference that can distract the target receiver.

(3) Once the message is received via the medium, the receiver must decode the creativity of the sender, which is heavily biased by their own perceptions, judgements and past experiences, to finally receive the message.

THE ART OF MARKETING

(4) After this, a response action is triggered, whether it be dismissal, negative, positive, purchase, and so on.

(5) Concluding the action, feedback from the receiver to the sender is sent, which must also go through the 'noise' or interference factor before the sender can use the data.

Different elements of the promotional mix approach this cycle in different ways. For example, personally selling is effective because it completes the cycle entirely in almost one transaction, whereas Public Relations campaigns are slower and can experience high amounts of noise.

Developing Effective Communication

(1) Identify the target audience

(2) Determine the objectives and goals of the communication message

(3) Design or encode the message creatively, catered to what would spark the interest of the target audience.

(4) Select appropriate channels

(5) Establish a budget for this message so as to determine best use of resources

(6) Determine which elements of the promotional mix to utilise

(7) Measure results

(8) Manage the IMC system

(9) Collect data on this experience to improve the next message

Reach and Frequency

When it comes to marketing communication strategy, reach and frequency are the two main factors that must be decided upon.

The reach is all about the level of access to the target market. How many segments within the target market need to be accessed? What times? What demographics? Which media do they use?

The frequency is about how many messages through those reach channels, above. If, for example, a magazine is the selected medium, then how many issues is the communication present in? How many times does the advertisement run on television? And so on.

There tends to be an "S"-shaped response curve that occurs with freq uency and effectiveness that all marketers must take into consideration. It is generally accepted that a low frequency of communications, such as between zero and three exposures, is not very effective at all. A medium frequency, above this, gains a high acceptance with the target market and thus is very effective (usually between three and ten rapid exposures). However a high frequency starts to lose its effectiveness and can even become negative if the target market becomes saturated and over-exposed to the content.

Advertising

Advertising, also known as paid-promotion or 'above the line' marketing is any communication message that is paid for by an organisation to a medium sponsor (such as a television station, a magazine, a bus shelter, a billboard, a radio station, and so on) that presents and promotes a product, non-personally. This means that it does not involve a personal, one-on-one interaction.

These kind of promotion offers the organisation almost complete control of the message as they can purchase a space and advertise however they'd like, within reason. This is usually the most expensive and competitive form however is extremely effective.

Marketers today, however, face a lot of challenges in advertising as there is a lot of noise and consumers are starting to filter out the 'same-old' advertising thrown constantly at them. As consumers are becoming more de-sensitised through over-exposure, marketers have to be far more creative to cater better and more effective messages to the target audience.

Marketers now tend to use different forms of advertising, such as 'crowd-sourcing', which is getting the target market actively involved in the advertising and creativity for a reward. This has large uptake by a target market as they feel involvement as worth their attention.

Advertising has five functions when being utilised: informing, persuading, reminding, adding value, assisting organisational efforts and favourability. One message can perform one or a combination of all of these functions. Favourability tends to be utilised more today- if a message is liked by an audience, it will tend to have more cut-through than an ad that rubs the audience the wrong way.

Public Relations (PR)

This is known as 'below-the-line' marketing and involves creating good relationships with the organisation's publics and stake-holders through favourable publicity, positive corporate and product image and managing or debunking unfavourable rumours, reviews and messages.

PR can be positive or negative and can function as an outlet for information or promotion, depending on the context. Unfortunately, PR isn't always in control by the organisation. Whilst some forms can be intentional, such as a press release, sometimes PR can be written or circulated without the knowledge of the organisation. Organisations such as Greenpeace tend to use witty PR campaigns to gain momentum for the causes within the community.

Event Sponsorship

Event sponsorship is a form of PR, where an organisation pays to be an official branded sponsor. This kind of PR allows for positive brand association with the event. However, for this to be a success, it is important that the product ties in well with the event- it can be a waste if there is no leverage by the organisation. Just a brand at an event isn't enough; there must be some related activity such as a stall at the event. A good sponsorship PR campaign capitalises by promoting the tie with the event.

However, with event sponsorship, 'ambush marketing' threatens to take advantage of such events. This is where an organisation will advertise with the event's theme unofficially so as to appear to be a sponsor and steal the limelight, when they're in fact not.

Experiential Marketing Campaign

A good way to gain positive PR is by letting customers trial a brand or product as an experience so that they consume the brand in a favourable experience setting and then share this with the market. For example, wine tasting in a beautiful vineyard or sports drinks during a volleyball game on the beach.

Sampling is another similar example of this, where consumers are given access to free trials to promote the product and break through distrust barriers.

Sales Promotion

Sales promotion is a short-term incentive given to customers to spur and increase purchase behaviour, such as the push and pull strategies discussed above. These can come in the form of discounts, buy-one-get-one free, coupons, lotteries, competitions and so on.

It is important, however, than an organisation avoids the sales promotion trap, which is over-incentivising to a point where the discount becomes the norm and the organisation can no longer remove the promotion.

Diverting can also occur. This is where someone or an organisation avoids the restrictions of a sales promotion, purchases these discounted goods in one region, and then sells in a non-discounted region.

Direct Marketing

This type of promotion began with physical mail marketing and has evolved to email and mobile phone marketing. Basically, it is any form of advertising that utilises an interactive media to gain a measurable result and response at any location.

Unfortunately, direct marketing tends to bombard consumers, so a good 'call to action' together with something that sparks the interest and curiosity of the target market enough to get them to respond.

The Internet's Role In Marketing

The internet is a fantastic resource for marketing efforts. It can perform the following functions for an organisation:

- Public relations
- Investor communications
- Customer service
- Prospect qualification
- Product sales
- Customer interaction and feedback
- Internal communications
- E-Commerce

It is very important that the use of the internet is consistent with the marketing strategy as, because it can perform so many simultaneous functions at once, all must be correctly utilised and managed to ensure a united front and message (a good IMC).

The internet's use has shifted greatly from simple websites to completely out-of-the-square marketing efforts such as interactive social media campaigns, mobile device marketing and so on.

LEVEL OF PERSONALISED CONTENT

It's not a coincidence anymore that, when browsing for that new sports watch, suddenly you're seeing ads for FitBit everywhere. It's not by chance that your research into real estate has triggered banner ads popping up all over your Facebook feed telling you to click to see the Commonwealth Bank's new mortgage package. It's not selective sight seeing ads for ASOS beckoning you back after shopping on their online store after abandoning your cart before purchase.

The internet is a very smart creature today, and has reached a level of targeting that transcends anything seen before. What I'm talking about here is the technique of Retargeting.

What Is Retargeting?

Retargeting (also sometimes referred to as remarketing) is responsible for the phenomena mentioned above. Basically, it facilitates re-engagement from a customer after they've left a brand's website.

Retargeting gathers a specific person's buying preferences, and then shows them targeted online adverts as they surf the net, to keep those relevant brands in front of them. The majority of customers (around 98%) who visit a website will actually leave (known as "bounce") before completing a purchase or performing a converting action. Retargeting addresses this by leveraging purchase intent data from that website (such as likes, shopping cart behaviour, history, time on site, clicks, and so on), and placing a small piece of code as a cookie on their browser, so that when they visit retargeting provider pages like Facebook, the individual is served ads tailored specifically for them.

This is a very effective marketing tool as it allows powerful, precisely targeted ads to be directed to each specific customer, encouraging them back to the original website to complete their transaction and convert.

Part Of A Larger Campaign

Obviously, this works best as part of an overall digital Marketing campaign. After all, you need customers to already know about your brand and visit your website for the first time as a result of an overarching promotion campaign, before you can effectively utilise retargeting to nurture and make them feel comfortable about returning to your website and trusting your brand. Retargeting is a good way to bolster this larger campaign.

Don't Frustrate Your Customers

Retargeting, however, requires a very delicate balance. It should be a complementary execution to your marketing mix, not an endless annoyance to your customers. Serving the wrong ad to the wrong person too many times (over bombardment) is the negative side of retargeting, and must be avoided. Retargeting works most effectively when it's a subtle, top-of-mind reminder, and not a hounding series of propaganda.

The ideal point is when the individual views the retargeted ads as a convenience, where ads are catered to their specific needs, rather than harassment, with ads stalking them around the internet. It's important to get this delicate balance correct.

The Multiplatform Scope

An effective retargeting strategy must span across many platforms, given the nature of the consumer today. These include desktops, mobile devices and social media. Most customers own multiple devices and will research on one platform, only to complete their transaction and post feedback on another, so retargeting must be reaching them via a multi-platform approach.

Get The Most Out Of Retargeting

Effectively using Retargeting lies in segmentation, creative design, experimentation and measurement.

Segmentation puts the right strategies in place to ensure the correct messages are delivered to the right consumer.

For example, a loyal customer will require a different type of message to one that is still unsure about purchasing. Correct segmentation ensures that a converted customer receives loyalty campaigns and cross selling messages, whereas a non-converted customer receives discounts and reassuring messages to bring them back to the site.

Creative design on retargeting adverts work best when they're kept simple and bold, display the brand prominently, have a direct call to action, and present a personalised message. After all, if you're going to all the trouble of individualising your Marketing massaging, don't waste the opportunity to connect directly with your customer.

Experiment with different designs, fre☐uencies, locations and landing pages to discover what gets the best result. As it is a specifically targeted campaign, it's often difficult to determine what resonates best with an individual segment.

Effective measurement is always key when determining the success of each marketing endeavour. Retargeting can meet customer retention, brand awareness and sales objectives, and the most commonly uses statistics to track progress are "Cost Per Action" and "Cost Per Clicks".

This was just an introduction into Retargeting. It's a very vast area and worth exploring in more detail before setting out on your own campaign. But the results speak for themselves. Good luck.

MARKETING MANAGEMENT

Before you get to understand what marketing management is it is important to understand what marketing is first. In layman's language marketing is the act of nurturing customer relations, preferably those that are profitable to the organization or firm. In the business world it is important for you to know the various terminologies used and how to apply them. Marketing management can be described as the thinking part of it. It seeks to describe the various aspects of the customer. Marketing is not just about advertising and making sells, it is about getting the customer's satisfaction.

It is very hard to run an organization without all the skills of marketing and management. That's why most successful individuals go for an introduction to marketing management. It is a course that will provide you with all the statistical skills of organizing and solving organizations problems. Marketing management involves many channels and forms. There are various aspects that have to be looked at when managing the marketing strategies of a particular firm.

The first thing you need to consider is the potential of the company that is what the firm has to offer. This should not be viewed in terms of the products only but also the services it can provide. Where most business people get it all wrong is that they put all their efforts in the business and end up forgetting about the customers' needs. This does not help in marketing the company's products since it should be seen from a customer's point, how the product is benefiting the customer. You need to understand all your customers' needs and satisfactions. You expectations should be to meet the customers' needs. Having full understanding of the customers' needs and implementing strategies to meet their demands will build a good customer relationship.

During marketing your goal should not only to win more customers but also to maintain them. This is achieved after building a good customer relation. If you come up with good products and services then there is no doubt that you will be able to get more customers and also maintain old ones.

In marketing management you should have a defined marketing channel for example you can have cross channel marketing where two forms of marketing supporting each other. A good example is a website and a catalogue. You can also use multi channel marketing where different marketing channels support each other. For example prints and a radio station that both advertise your websites and your products.

If you are marketing your company through a website then there are certain things you need to understand about internet marketing. For internet marketing you should start by having a good domain name, the next thing is optimizing your websites through the search engines for you to create traffic to your website.

Now that you have had an introduction to marketing management it is upon you to take these challenges and put them into action for you to realize desirable profits. As much as it may not be that easy but it is worth the challenge.

DIGITAL VS TRADITIONAL MARKETING

Where do we spend our precious budget to get the most cut through to engage our audiences and achieve our organisational goals?

So, it's finally time to analyse both sides and get to the bottom of this debate.

Where Are Our Customers?

Effective Marketing is all about your audience. This is never up for dispute as we all know it to be true. Knowing that, it may be time to take a step back and consider that age old question: have we thought about our customer?

Recent research shows that 87% of consumers now search online for reviews to determine the quality of a local business, and I'm sure that statistic is pretty similar for how people are researching product information too. This is a big shift in behaviour from only a couple of years ago. Organisations didn't start this- consumers did. We did. We, as people, changed the game, and organisations today are hugely naïve if they don't think people are already doing most of their research before even contacting your business.

As An Example

Prince said his son needed an internet router for his house the other day, and at first, he had no clue what a router even was. In about ten minutes online, he become a pro with all of the brands, prices and specifications, then went straight into a local store, went to the shelf and purchased it without speaking to anyone in store.

This is very indicative of the modern customer.

The Digital Interview

Today, it's all about 'the digital interview'- in other words, searching online to find more information about a person or business without actually contacting them. Online dating, LinkedIn, Facebook, websites- it's all about research before meeting in person. Around 70% of customers make up their mind before that stage, which is something businesses need to accept and adapt to.

While statistics are always fickle, all you need to do is think about your own customer's behaviour, and you instantly know this to be true. Hardly ever does a customer go in unprepared or uninformed.

They're All Online

THE ART OF MARKETING

How often do we go to a bar or a restaurant, and find everyone looking at a screen? It's a sad reality, but a reality none the less. That is where your customer is! On their digital device.

People aren't looking for reviews and information in your physical office or in your marketing collateral - they are looking online. So, being there for your audience is absolutely crucial for your business success.
It's all about your audience, after all.

The Three Arguments: Digital vs Traditional Marketing

There are the three main considerations when deciding the pros and cons of new digital marketing versus more traditional methods, like the letter box drop or print.

(1) Cost
(2) Effectiveness
(3) Accountability

COST

As a general rule, more traditional methods tend to be far more costly in so many ways. It's expensive to design, print and physically deliver materials like these. Now look at digital methods: it's almost instant, re□uires little design due to templates, and the reach is not physically limited, meaning you can get ten times the exposure for around one-tenth of the cost.

They seem to be light years apart on the cost front.

For example, a client came to me recently and told me that the only advertising he was doing was on the back of local shopper dockets, which wasn't giving him any tangible results, but was still costing him a few hundred dollars a month. For a fraction of this cost, I put his adverts onto Facebook and Google, and he immediately noticed the difference in leads generated!

EFFECTIVENESS

How long do letterbox drops, print media and even mainstream advertising last?
Think about a letterbox specifically. The printed material sits in an office, then in a mail box all day. Then, when your audience gets home, are they truly engaged when they check their letterbox, stumbling in from work? They are coming home with the shopping, or wrangling the kids. This material has literally one second to capture them in amongst the rest of the clutter, and is so easy to ignore. That's not to say it doesn't occasionally work, but the chance of engagement is very low.

Now, consider digital ads. It stays online for a much longer time, and due to the customisable nature of online targeting, it can pop up when the customer is more engaged and in the right headspace. It meets them on their terms, like when they are on their phone killing time, or browsing on a website, and so on. They can also interact with it by clicking on it, watching it, zooming in on it, saving it and much more.

In comparison, think about when you hear a radio ad or see a TV ad: you have to remember and recall the advert at a later time for it to have any impact. This means your audience has to spend the effort to remember to act on it at a later time when it's more relevant, such as when they get out of the car. Making this worse today is that we are constantly bombarded by ads and messages, which means that it's very hard to keep one specific advert in your mind. You can't rely on your customer recalling the message - you need to make it easy and at their fingertips.

Digitally, your customer can fully interact at the very point they experience the piece of content, meaning engagement is far greater.

ACCOUNTABILITY

Which technique truly works? What really has cut through and metrics to measure it? If you ask most organisations who spend budget yearly on letterbox drops, for example, they will say things like "$50,000 a year", and then if you ask them "does this work?", all they do is shrug their shoulders.

The problem is, some businesses get into a rut of "it's how we've always done it." This represents a concerning shortfall in our perspective and our priorities. Our industries are too tough and our competitors too smart for us to be thinking this way anymore.

On the digital marketing side, with retarget marketing and tracking cookies, online communication and adverts are able to serve up your communication to more defined and far better aligned demographics. Your adverts are more intelligent because they learn about the behaviour of your audience and adapt to how they consume content, then works out where and when to best display your marketing.

The Three Battlegrounds of Marketing

From the 1960ies, there has been an evolution of Marketing and communication battlegrounds based on how we built our customer database.

> (1) The Physical Address
>
> Organisations clambered to obtain the physical addresses of customers to communicate with them physically, either with a sales person, door knocking or letter box communications.

(2) The Email Address

Next, emails went through an effective stage and businesses rushed to fill their databases with everyone's @.com address. However today, we have found this to be far less effective do the □uantity of spam everyone receives daily.

(3) The Computer Address

People live on their mobiles and tablets now- this is where they are today. The battlefield has become exposure based on IP address online. Building a database of tracking cookies has become the Marketing battleground of today.

While these IP addresses are kept private due to Privacy Laws and you never get the actual details, it doesn't matter as you can rest assured that this technology is getting your message in front of the right people. Then tracking success comes from the metrics and analytics behind these interactions.

The core essence of Marketing hasn't changed across any of the above battlegrounds: it's always been about reaching your audience. The only thing that has changes is how- and this is a direct result from how the marketplace and consumer behaviour is evolving.

THE ART OF MARKETING

What is it about Digital Marketing then?

Digital Marketing is effective because it is customisable. It can target specific demographics to ensure that the best audience is getting your adverts and content at the right times.

The following are three combined ways of how digital marketing finds your audience.

(1) Location

Google tags computers with a geographical location. While letterbox drops can do the same, location is where the comparison ends. Digital is able to combine location with the following two ⬚ualifiers to ensure that your message is tailored, rather than mass distributed to just anyone.

For example, in the Real Estate industry, around 70% of residences are investor controlled, which means letterbox drops are ineffective because the people receiving the materials are not the decision makers and therefore not finding themselves in the hands of the right people. Digital equivalents would use location and the following two to ensure it is being fed to the right customers.

(2) Browsing History

It is the fact above that allows digital marketing to take it one step further. The history of your browser paints a picture of the type of person your customer is and their interests, which means that adverts can be served up to match this. It's not a perfectly accurate science, however due to the cost effectiveness of digital marketing, it has a far better cut through and success rate.

(3) Remarketing and Tracking Cookies

As you move from website to website, tracking cookies embed themselves into your web browser to allow the content be catered specifically to you, so you are not receiving irrelevant messages. This allows advertising content to be shown to a relevant audience rather than just anyone.

Where is Marketing Heading Next?

Given that digital marketing is following around your ideal customer and delivering them relevant content, it seems to be working effectively at the moment. However, if I know Marketing the way I think I do, the next stage will be empathetic retarget marketing, which means showing the advert not just anywhere on any website, but when the person is browsing material that is contextually relevant.

For example, when your customer, who has already been identified as interested in Real Estate, reaches a Real Estate or property website, the ad will be displayed, as opposed to how it is now, where it comes up on any website they may be looking at.

It's all about being in front of the right customer when they are in the right frame of mind.

WHAT MARKETING AUTOMATION MEANS?

The act of automating these steps with the help of technology and software turns it into Marketing Automation.

Thus, when with the help of a business software some or many steps of marketing are handled automatically by a software or application, that's called marketing automation.

Beginning of Marketing Automation

So, at the beginning, when computer and internet were new and weren't matured as much as they are today, the marketing companies used to compile a long list of prospective clients and then send them the same mail one by one. Then someone invented a function by which people were able to enlist all email IDs in one email and send a bulk email.

We can call that the first Marketing Automation attempt as the system had automated one part of the marketing campaign. Now there was no need to send each individual one by one. It was now done with a single click. Though, you had to create a database of all the email IDs first, but the repetitive process of composing the same email for every individual was discarded.

From the that time on, people have just built upon the same idea, transformed more manual steps into the automatic ones and more and more repetitive efforts performed by executives has turned into automated ones.

Today, it is possible to send one mail to a thousand (or a million) people without writing a single word, without entering email IDs manually or hitting send at the moment you want send it.

How? A few types of mails have readymade formats available for free. You can take that format as the body of your mail. Then there are services which provide you list of email IDs in the domains you require. And then on an email client, you schedule your emails to automatically be sent without your presence. See? Nothing is written and yet you have sent thousands of emails with a few clicks.

Though, such email with readymade templates will have a very low conversion rate. Yet, it reflects the reach and advancements in the marketing automation segment. You are only re□uired to tell the software what you want to do and then, everything is done automatically.

Marketing Automation: Intelligence Gathering

Marketing Automation software has gone advanced and thus they have also made the every steps of marketing advanced. The aforementioned simple formula of marketing has become complex, much more focused, centralized and aligned for the maximum ROI. Nowadays, only gathering lists of email IDs isn't enough. For maximum efficiency you have more software and techniques to discard the people and steps which have less possibility to turn into conversion. You can target only those people who have higher likability of turning into a customer.

How you/software know that?

Today, in the times of matured internet with the social media sites, increased internet footprints, there is software available which follows and tracks a person's internet footprint on social media, search engines, different websites and all the things they click and look out for on the internet. After that, the software segmentizes the data and turns it into actionable information. Basing on that information, the tool suggests you the people which are most likely to convert into customer as they are probably following the similar things which falls into the product category of your product or their interests and search results suggests that they are interested into the product you are selling i.e. a person running a big firm is more likely to buy your CRM (Customer Relationship Management) system than a man who sells candies at a local shop. Thus, you can discard the people who aren't going to buy your product and focus only on the people with higher likability. This way, your spending on mail clients shows higher ROI with maximum efficiency. The rate of replies, mail openings, leads and ultimately to the conversion also stays high.

Thus, the software and tools are helping to maximize your performance by intelligence gathering from online sites and people's online footprints. Collected intelligence is helping you to do marketing efficiently, smartly and with higher return.

Marketing Automation: Workflow Automation inside the Company

There is this third part of the marketing automation which furthers the game to the next level which makes sure that you are always there to close the deal for any customer who is interested in your product. It's called Workflow Automation.

Workflow Automation actually tracks the performance of the recent marketing campaign and sees if the prospect has reached to a level where he is considering buying your product. He is probably visiting your website regularly, spends longer time on it or is visiting the product pricing page. At that time, the marketing automation software understands the prospect's higher possibility of turning into a conversion. At that critical time, the software sends to one of your marketing executive an alert for such a prospect who, from there on, can take predefined steps to ensure the prospect turns into a conversion. The Marketing Automation Software are looking at the people's profiles, habits, nature and collective psychographic data to understand if he will be interested in your product or not.

> *That's marketing automation at its maximum performance.*

You can understand that all the marketing automation tricks, techniques and ways described here are just the extensions of the decades old basic marketing formula. Those three steps are now highly matured with their own sub-parts, polished to a level where the conversion ration stays high, with segmented information about the prospects to target only the best ones and achieve results with far higher leads and conversions than its basic counterpart.

> *Marketing Automation isn't only for Email Marketing.*

That's true. Whenever a person thinks of online marketing, email marketing pops up the first. But, as its well-known, there are a lot of other ways to market your product online. Social media posts, online conferences/calls/webinars, website promotion, advertisements, etc. There are a lot of options and each one is a marketing effort.

Now, in each of these techniques, if there is a Marketing Automation Software available which is making a few steps automatic i.e. posting on multiple social media sites at once or posting articles/press releases automatically on multiple article directories or article/PR submission sites, then that software is helping in your marketing campaign and is making it automatic. That is also a marketing automation software.

- Marketing Automation isn't bound only to email marketing.

How to know if you require a marketing automation software?

The criteria is simple. If you rely on email marketing, social media marketing and other traceable online marketing techniques, then here are the situations to use a marketing automation software:

- If you are repetitively sending thousands and thousands of emails to your prospect on daily/weekly/monthly basis
- You require a detailed review of your marketing campaign
- Using a software reduces cost/time/efforts spent on the task greatly

Benefits

Benefits of marketing automation are:

- It accelerates the whole campaign tremendously

- Marketing Intelligence helps you to target only prospects with higher conversion possibility
- Your employees get great support to track down and assist the most interested prospect. Thus, it goes to the last mile to ensure one more deal is closed.
- The detailed analytics and statistics help you to get better and better with your every campaign

WHAT CAN MARKETING MAKE YOU?

When it comes to business, spending money on things with an unpromised, unspecified or uncertain return is a tough pill to swallow. Most business owners budget very carefully - they want to know what they're spending their money on and why; how their money is working for them. Marketing is one of those gray areas where, especially for the not-totally-new-school business owner, it can be difficult to grasp the concept of allocating large amounts of dollars toward something you only hope will work in the end.

That's why a business mindset of scarcity is much more common than one of abundance - because when the results are unpredictable, it's easier to just stick with what you've got. But instead of asking, "what will marketing cost me?" more business owners are exploring the possibilities that emerge when they ask, "what will marketing make me?" And I'm here to tell you.

The reason why more companies (and small businesses in particular) are opening up their minds - and their wallets - to a new way of thinking is because they have most likely found at least one of the following five things to be true:

1. Marketing Makes You Money

Sure, marketing costs money. But it's not supposed to be a blindfolded spend frenzy. If you know enough about marketing to test the waters with some high-value organic techniques that will get you a lot of mileage, then go for it, by all means. This will help inform your strategy down the road so that you have an idea of the areas where you need help, and so that you can reasonably predict your marketing expenditure.

However, if you seek the advice of a professional, the right marketer will set your mind at ease by not expecting you to dump huge amounts of money into their accounts up front and by explaining each strategy they propose, as well as why they're priced the way they are. Then they'll put together a ☐uote which should not only align with your goals, but illustrate the anticipated return in proportion to the suggested spend.

Let's face it, 'marketing' is a broad term but, in essence, the purpose of any marketing strategy is to get you found. Your product or service will only make you money if it is used by people, and awareness precedes use, wouldn't you say? Whether you employ digital marketing methods such as building a great website, blogging, email marketing, social media, and paid ads; or go old-school with direct mail, circular ads, door-to-door advertising, and cold-calling, the intent is the same: get people to buy from you.

Marketing, when done right, should bring opportunities to your sales force, traffic to your website, and rings to your phone. Ask yourself: if you don't have a website, then how are you getting found? How long will your current strategy be sustainable? Will it help you grow? If you have a website but it's not bringing you business, then it isn't working. Word of mouth success is wonderful, but do you have a plan in place for customer retention and acquisition? The answer shouldn't be "how much will marketing cost me?" but rather, "how much do I want to make and how can marketing get me there?"

2. Marketing Makes You Reputable

How many times have you visited an establishment based on a word-of-mouth recommendation from a friend? Probably quite a few. Ever been somewhere really fantastic that you wouldn't have otherwise selected if not for a positive review? Exactly! It doesn't matter if people love your business if they're not spreading the word, and a digital presence makes it much easier for your great reviews to be found by the masses. Publishing testimonials and success stories on your website is a wonderful way to market yourself and show prospects that they can trust your brand just like other customers have. Furthermore, getting yourself listed on well-known and highly trafficked directory sites makes it easy for people to do their homework before they buy - which is an integral part of the customer satisfaction experience.

3. Marketing Makes You Credible

Not to be confused with reputation, credibility is a major factor in many buyers' decisions. How do you distinguish yourself from competitors? What makes you more of an expert on your particular field or subject area? What sets your product apart? Well, don't tell me - tell the world! You need a platform from which you can showcase your skills, expertise, or must-have product.

Blogging and social media marketing are excellent ways to use your own unique voice to educate buyers and demonstrate thought leadership without always delivering an overtly hard sell. People like information, and they're more likely to trust you if the information you provide is relevant to their problems, needs and experiences in such a way that makes them want to come back and keep getting information from you (instead of just hearing your sales pitch and then leaving to continue shopping around elsewhere). This is especially vital for less well-known companies that don't have as much publicized feedback or presence. In order to stand up against your competitors, you must demonstrate credibility.

4. Marketing Makes You Accessible

It's one thing to have a website. But if you're just starting out or if no one knows your name, it's not enough to just have a website. How are you driving traffic to that website? Waiting and hoping are not measurable techniques that deliver results. You need a strategy, and you need SEO.

Maybe you've heard of search engine optimization (surely you've used that little thing called Google). Basically, SEO is tied into the design and function of your website so that search engines (like Google) can display your content to people who are looking for related information. If your website isn't optimized, then it's just sitting there. Sure, someone can type your URL and probably even search for your business name on Google - if they know your name. But if you've got a niche product or service or you're brand new to an area, no one will know to do that. You need your company or product to pop up in the search results whenever someone types in "Philadelphia wedding photographer," or "men's custom tailored vintage suits" (you get the idea).

5. Marketing Makes You Attractive

This should be self-explanatory. Let's be honest, we do tend to judge books by their covers, and we are (even if ever so slightly) biased toward companies - and people - who present themselves well. Marketing and branding are all around you. If you're anything like me, you're a sucker for the pretty packaging in the cosmetics aisle at Target (or the highly visible promise of a product that does it all, is portable, and comes with a warranty).

The same goes for your brand identity, whether you're a large organization or a music teacher! The way you present yourself to the masses will play an important role in the amount of opportunity that converts to business. Online presence is becoming so important that it's almost unacceptable to have a sub-par website. For people who still use business cards (and who aren't constrained by corporate marketing guidelines), being memorable and capturing someone's attention with a 3.5-inch piece of paper re☐uires some creativity. What's on the cover is not always a measure of what's inside, but the cover should at least make someone want to open the book. The way your business appears to others is a reflection of the way your business will eventually appear to your banker.

Lack of Marketing Costs You Everything

Short of ☐uoting JFK for emphasis, there's really no other way I can say it (you got it, right? Please tell me you got it). Don't wait around doing cost analysis and pinching pennies. While you're doing that, your competition is outperforming you. A marketing strategy doesn't have to cost thousands. Figure out what you can spend and shop around. Start small: any improvement is a good investment. You can always scale up when your initial investment pays off.

Of course, marketing isn't the only ingredient for success. You should also deliver great customer service, quality, value, and purpose. Marketing attracts customers, but it's your responsibility to keep them around. Remember - the internet provides complete freedom of speech. Once you build a presence, it will be just as easy for people to find negative feedback about you if it exists. In this way, let a marketing strategy hold you accountable to your business for stepping up your game in every way. You owe it to your company, and perhaps even your livelihood.

So, in short, become easy to find, add content that makes people glad they found you, let the world know how satisfied your customers are, and present your business in the most appealing way possible and you'll see why a focused marketing strategy pays off more than sticking to the status □uo. You and your business can become these five things and more - just embrace it!

WHY SALES AND MARKETING MUST ALIGN

Let's talk about a sales and marketing problem most companies have struggled with for years. I'm not talking about lead generation, market share, or customer retention, although it does impact each of those things and so much more. I'm talking about the chasm that separates Sales and Marketing.

Take a look at a typical day in the life of both Sales and Marketing to see if you can relate...

A Day in the Life of a Marketer

A marketer works hard to generate leads for her sales team. She optimizes conversion opportunities across her company's website, delivers email campaigns, builds landing pages and delivers valuable gated content. Her work generates a steady stream of leads, which she immediately passes along to the sales team. Because, after all, more leads is better, right?

Our marketer toils away each day to create valuable marketing content and sales support materials. She sends emails to the sales team to notify them each new piece of content as it is finalized. She even uploads each new item to the company's Dropbox account so everyone can access it.

Ah, sweet success!

But not for long...

Her blood boils when she learns her sales reps haven't even so much as looked at the leads she has been generating. She shivers with frustration when she finds out most of the sales team is somehow unaware of most of the content she has created. How can this be possible?

Marketing feels undervalued and ignored.

A Day in the Life of a Sales Rep

On the other side of the Grand Sales and Marketing Canyon, a sales rep spends her day responding to urgent prospect requests, traveling from meeting to meeting, communicating with customers, reacting to unexpected changes with buyers - hers is a life of constant chaos and change.

She often needs content in order to respond to immediate needs of her prospects. However, this leads to frustration because the materials she has access to are not the materials she needs. They are outdated or - worse yet - they don't even seem to exist. This often means she ends up creating content on the spot. This requires time she simply doesn't have. She can't understand why Marketing doesn't produce the content she needs.

To top it off she receives endless notifications from Marketing about new leads she to follow up with, adding pressure to her already stress-filled day. She doesn't have time to stay on top of communication with her own prospects, let alone a list of new leads from Marketing. Besides, Marketing leads never seem to be qualified and following up with them always seems to be a waste of her time.

Sales feels misunderstood and unsupported by Marketing.

Sound familiar? Yeah, I thought so.

Unfortunately, this situation is incredibly common. Marketers are not alone in their feelings of being undervalued and ignored. In fact, as much as 80% of marketing leads will never be acted upon by Sales. And according to the American Marketing Association, a whopping 90% of selling content is never actually used in selling.

Sales reps, too, are justified in their frustration. The CMO council found that instead of selling, sales people spend upwards of 40% of their time creating their own messaging and tools. Also, according to HubSpot, only 27% of leads sent to sales by marketing are qualified first.

Pretty sad statistics, right? So why is it happening? It's that chasm I mentioned earlier between Sales and Marketing. These two teams are disconnected in a big way and it's taking a toll on the companies they work for.

It's time to close the gap and align Sales and Marketing once and for all. While you would probably agree, you may not fully understand why it's so important or what you can do about it.

Why Sales and Marketing MUST Align

Reason #1: Your Customers See It

According to the IDC, as much as 57% of customers feel that salespeople are poorly prepared or not prepared at all for initial meetings.

Could it be that these sales reps didn't have the resources they needed to properly prepare for these initial meetings? After all, these meetings with prospective customers are pretty important to sales reps - they are key milestones in the sales process! The vast majority of sales reps would certainly want to be prepared for them so they could be as successful as possible. They just didn't have the content they needed to adequately prepare.

Sales reps need content to effectively engage prospects and close sales. But not just any content will do. They need content that speaks directly to the needs, challenges and preferences of prospects. And they need to be able to access the most current versions of it whenever they need it.

What To Do

Take the first step toward Sales and Marketing alignment and talk to the sales reps directly. Work to clearly understand the challenges they face throughout the sales process. Ask them about the gaps they see in your marketing content. Try to understand how they need to access content and when and where they need it most. Attempt to learn what marketing support has worked and what has not - and why. Listen to their feedback and list the ways you can better serve your sales reps.

One strategy I like to use is asking sales reps to write down questions they frequently receive from prospects. Then, use this list of FAQs as a list of content you can create to directly support the sales reps the next time they encounter such inquiries.

The important takeaway here is that marketers can take the first step toward Sales and Marketing alignment by starting a simple conversation with sales reps. Just ask them what they need and work out a way to deliver it.

Reason #2: Lead Overload

When Sales and Marketing aren't aligned, inefficiencies are bound to happen. Like the examples given above, chances are pretty good that Marketing is delivering leads that Sales will never touch. With increasing adoption of marketing automation platforms and their ability to help marketers do more than ever before, marketers are capable of generating a lot of leads. That's great. What's not so great is when they just pass them all along to sales.

Why is this such a problem? When sales reps are given more leads than they are physically able to follow up with, they become saturated... and those leads get neglected Here's an example:

Let's say you've been striving to reach a lead generation goal of 30 leads per rep per week. That sounds great! That is, until you learn that each rep typically has about two hours per week to follow up with leads and each lead typically requires about 20 minutes of follow up time. You now realize that each rep has the capacity to follow up with just six leads each week. You have been working hard to send them 30.

See the problem here? In this scenario, you would be sending them 24 more leads than they can physically handle. Every. Single. Week.

What you thought was great marketing success was actually overloading sales. And it was leading to neglected leads.

What To Do

As the previous example briefly mentioned, one of the first steps in solving this problem is by talking to your sales reps and Sales leadership directly to understand the realistic number of leads each rep can follow up with each week. Then adjust the number of leads you deliver accordingly.

This doesn't mean you aim try to generate fewer leads. Not at all. Instead, it means you might need to nurture them and better ◻ualify them before handing them off to Sales.

More work for marketing? Perhaps. But wouldn't it be worth it if your work was actually used? By nurturing leads before handing them off to Sales, you increase the chances of the leads you deliver actually becoming customers.

On average, according to a Demand Gen Report nurtured leads produce a 20% increase in sales opportunities versus non-nurtured leads. What's more, companies that excel at lead nurturing generate 50% more leads that are truly sales-ready. Even better - they produce these leads a third of the cost of companies that aren't so great at lead nurturing.

Invest some time in better understanding Sales and each rep's capacity for following up with leads. Then refine your lead nurturing process to improve the quality and rethink the quantity of leads you deliver to sales.

Reason #3: Revenue Gone to Waste

When sales reps spend time searching for or creating content, this not only duplicates the efforts of marketing, it also pulls them away from important sales opportunities. And those wasted opportunities add up to wasted revenue - lots of it.

Consider this: A study by IDC found that by saving a single sales rep just 60 minutes of prep time each week, a company could realize additional revenue generation $300,000 or more per rep! In a company with just 10 reps, that's $3 million each year. If you've got 100 reps, that's a staggering $300MM per year.

If just 60 minutes of prep time can translate into $300,000 in revenue, just imagine how much potential revenue is wasted in your organization as sales reps struggle to find the content they need.

What To Do

Clear out the clutter. As you work to build a better relationship with your sales reps and establish more freΩuent, meaningful communication, look for ways you can reduce the clutter - in both of your lives.

Quite often, technology can help here. There are apps available today to help manage content. Anything from Google Drive to Basecamp, Dropbox to Salesforce - any number of tools can serve as a virtual marketing library for your content. Each one is available anywhere and on any device with an internet connection so sales reps should have no problem getting the content they need whenever they need it.

If you can commit to making only the most current versions of content available in this marketing library, ask your sales reps to also make a commitment. Ask them to retrieve these up-to-date versions of content whenever they need to use it - instead of using outdated content stored elsewhere or creating their own.

Close the gap between Sales and Marketing. Reach out to Sales to better understand their challenges and needs. Work together to better serve your customers. Sure, it will improve your business and probably increase revenue, but it will also improve your workplace happiness, and can you really put a price on that?

COMMON MARKETING MISTAKES

If you are one of the small business operators who would like to do better than the average competitor, then this eBook is for you. Here are my six common mistakes that many small business owners make and switched on operators should avoid.

No Marketing Plan

Can you easily locate an up-to-date plan of how you are going to market your business over the next six months? Failing to plan or planning to fail?

While planning a marketing strategy is often thought of as something reserved solely for big business, it is equally applicable or even more critical for small business. Unlike bigger companies where a strategic error may not be as critical, a mistake made within a smaller company can put it out of business.

It is amazing how opportunities open up and become clearer during and after the marketing planning process. I recently completed a marketing plan for a fashion client where we identified both long- and short-term goals. To get some immediate 'money in the bank', we decided to have a sale to clear out a number of items that were sitting in the client's showroom, taking up space as well as restricting working capital.

The sale was highly successful and the small business owner was very pleased to have a few more thousand dollars in the bank account! I realise that this may seem ꓺuite an obvious thing to do, but it is often difficult to think of new ideas to promote your business and generate sales when you are the person involved in it, all day every day. An external supplier's point of view and fresh perspective can make the world of difference.

By failing to plan is planning to fail. By going through the marketing planning process a business can define, refine and fully communicate the product or service for itself, its team and for its customers. By doing so, a business can understand the strengths of what it does and how to apply these into real business situations.

Not Knowing Who Your Target Audience Is

Can you define specifically for each product and/or service in your business, who your target audience is?

All of the savvy and smart marketing decisions are based on knowing and specifically understanding who your target audience is. Be as narrow as possible in your definition - having fewer people to market to can be a strong advantage.

For example, if you are a gym your overall product offer is fitness. At various times of the day, however, a gym attracts different types of clientele - during the day your clients may be mums and retired people, whereas the afternoon and before work times may be more suited to young professionals. Both groups are using the same equipment and perhaps have similar motivations; however, each group has different needs and hot buttons when it comes to using a gym.

Marketing campaigns should be created for each target audience group and tailored to their individual requirements where possible. As demonstrated above, one size does not fit all.

No One Assigned to Marketing

Can you identify one person in your business that is responsible and accountable for marketing?

If everyone is responsible for marketing in your business, then no one actually is. Marketing by committee also does not work. While it is important to take into account various points of view, at the end of the day marketing is best assigned to one person who can be wholly accountable and responsible for the marketing function in your business.

Does having one person responsible for marketing work in big and small business? Looking back on a job I held a number of years ago as a marketing manager, I was the sole person responsible for marketing in that company. Though at times it was frustrating and isolating, I only realised what I had achieved in my role when I left that company. The evidence was in the fact that they ended up hiring three people to do my old job!

As a small business owner you may not have the luxury of being able to afford to hire a full-time senior marketing person. Nonetheless, it is important to make someone responsible for marketing regardless of whether that is a junior marketing assistant, yourself or an outsourced marketing supplier.

No Tracking Mechanisms

For each marketing campaign you have, do you have mechanisms in place for tracking results? In the era of digital communication, tracking campaigns will no doubt continue to become easier and more cost-effective. If there is no way to track your results easily and cost-effectively, do you really want to make an investment in a campaign where the results are based on gut feels?

My suggestions for ways to measure campaigns include:

- Unique URLs (website pages) - tracked through programs such as Google Analytics
- Use of virtual numbers for large campaigns

- Coupon codes, and
- Specific offers only available through one campaign

No Consistent Brand Templates

Do all of your business and marketing tools do justice to your logo and follow a style guide template?

The question is: does your branding appear consistently across all of your business and marketing tools. Things to check are business cards, invoices, letterhead, websites, blog pages, Yellow Pages, advertisements etc... It is very easy over a period of time to develop numerous templates in your business. The receptionist creates a fax form, your salesperson creates a sales follow-up letter and your accounts person creates a debt collection template, all of which have your name and logo on them, but may in fact look completely different.

Creating a strong and consistent brand template and following a strict style guide helps all the people in your business use your brand correctly. I recently worked with a client on creating a style guide as the imagery of the business had changed over a five-year period.

While all the changes were subtle, they became quite noticeable when observed from start to finish. Having a clear and consistent brand that is used correctly across all aspects of your business subtly tells your customers that your service offer is reliable and you are a strong, organised business.

Poor Copy/Text

Do you have an expert who can write text for your marketing tools?

When was the last time you went to a restaurant and spotted spelling mistakes on the menu? It is a common mistake and I see it at least once a week.

PILLARS OF MARKETING SUCCESS

Does the following give a pretty good picture of your current marketing activity?

You have a website but you're not really satisfied with it. You go to networking events once in awhile. If someone asks you to give a talk, you're happy to do it. You post on Facebook and/or LinkedIn semi-regularly. When you find the time, you send an article to those on your relatively small email list. You occasionally set up meetings with colleagues to explore opportunities.

Now there's nothing wrong with any of those marketing activities. And usually, they will result in landing some new clients.

But this is not the approach that works to get a steady, predictable stream of new clients.

Please don't tune me out here, thinking, "Well, I really can't do more than this. I'm already stretched thin. If you give me too much to do I'll get overwhelmed."

I agree. It's not that you need to do more marketing, it's that you need to shift your marketing paradigm from one of "Randomness" to one that is "Focused."

Random marketing is just that; it's all over the place. You do a little bit here and a little bit there on an inconsistent basis. You are trying to keep your face, name, and message in front of your prospective clients but the results are unpredictable.

The Random marketing paradigm is not very effective because it doesn't gain a lot of momentum. You don't do enough of one marketing activity to grab the attention of your prospective clients and move them to take action.

The Focused Marketing Paradigm is very different. It's based on repeatedly communicating very directly to your target market with a very definite end in mind. It gets the attention of your prospective clients and they ultimately take action.

The Focused Marketing Paradigm has Five Pillars

Understand and implement these five pillars and I promise you'll see a shift in your marketing results.

Pillar One: Focused Goals

A Random goal is saying something like, "I'd like to attract a few more clients to my business." Not very compelling is it?

A Focused goal is much more specific. "My goal is to land 3 new clients in the high-tech plastics business in the Houston area with an average project size of $30,000 each by the end of the year."

The more detail, depth, and specificity about the goal, the better. You've really thought through what you want to achieve and also have confidence that you could deliver if you did reach your goal. It's so real to you that you can taste it.

What is the Focused Goal for your marketing?

Pillar Two: Focused Program or Service

Random programs or services are generalized consulting, coaching or training programs. "I offer management consulting and training to corporations." Kind of vague, right? But this is what I hear all the time.

A Focused Program or Service is more tangible. "I offer the high-tech plastics industry Management Acceleration Programs for emerging leaders in the industry."

In my business, I've always offered programs: The Marketing Mastery Program, the Marketing Action Group, and the More Clients Club. And each program has very specific parameters, deliverables, and objectives. It sure makes intangible services easier to market and sell.

What is the Focused Program or Service you're offering?

Pillar Three: Focused Target Market

In the above example, the target was the "high-tech plastics industry." But it's more common to hear things like, "I work with large companies who want to increase productivity." This is too general and it makes it hard for clients to know if you understand them and can help them.

A Focused target market is where you are absolutely clear what kinds of people or companies can most benefit from your expertise. And then you articulate that clearly.

Who exactly is your Focused Target Market?

Pillar Four: Focused Message and Value Proposition

A Random message or value proposition tends to be too general and can be hard to pin down. It avoids making a promise that is meaningful to the prospective client.

Messages such as, "We offer the best service in the industry," or "Smart insights into great management," are meaningless to your prospective clients. The value is not immediately obvious.

A Focused message or value proposition zeros in on exactly what your clients get and what it means to them. I admit that this can be the marketing pillar that is hardest to pin down. Ultimately you have to test a number of different things.

For the re-launch of the More Clients Club, my current value proposition is: "Everything Self-Employed Professionals Need in One Place to Attract More Clients." And now, of course, I'm bending over backward to deliver on that promise.

And a marketing message or value proposition is much more than a sound bite. Your message must permeate every aspect of your marketing, from your website to the emails you send out. Your prospects need to be constantly reminded of the value you offer.

What is your Focused Message or Value Proposition?

Pillar Five: Focused Marketing Strategy

A Random marketing strategy is much like the collection of marketing activities I outlined at the top of the article. You're just all over the place, throwing something at the wall, hoping it will stick, with no organized system or plan.

A Focused marketing strategy is more like a putting on a theatrical production. You have the script, the actors, rehearsals, and opening night, all executed on a strict timeline.

That's the power of a focused marketing strategy.

You need to identify the right marketing strategy for your business, but even more important is the way you organize and implement the strategy.

Developing a focused strategy is the most complex and challenging of the Five Pillars. You can't just put together something haphazardly and hope you get the equivalent of a professional Shakespearian production.

What is your Focused Marketing Strategy?

If you work to build a focused plan with these five solid pillars, your marketing will work better and faster, attracting more of your ideal clients, usually at a higher rate.

WHY IS DIGITAL MARKETING SO IMPORTANT

Why is digital marketing so important?

The next big hopes for the best results in business development and career growth.

As the internet users across the world have been increased massively by year on year and when it compares to since 2000-2018 the ratio is increasing year by year. Now the fifty percent (50%) of the population around the world are using the internet. And by 2020 the active internet users are crossing 65% of the population across the world.

The main reason to increase the active internet users in last few years is due to the high usage of smartphones, tablets, and other smart devices around the world. These are very handy and useful to carry along with people where ever they go. Considering all these points the online marketing is a vast and broadly open to all the people around the world to connect through multiple devices like (Mobile (Smartphone), Laptop, Desktop, Tablet, Smart TV etc.) So this is going to help the Digital Marketing industry to expand worldwide their online market everywhere without having any shops in a particular place.

Now let us know the importance and the advantages of Digital Marketing.

The important thing in the digital marketing it is very easy to adapt and connect with the target audience worldwide. There are multiple chapters under digital marketing category which is coming with different modules. A few prime modules details have been briefly given below for the reference.

The prime chapters in digital marketing courses

1 Websites (for online presence)
2 Content Marketing
3 SEO/ Search Engine Optimization
4 Google Ads
5 Social Media Marketing/ Facebook, Twitter, LinkedIn, Instagram etc.
6 Email Marketing
7 Mobile Marketing
8 Social Media Optimization
9 Online Reputations Management
10 Analytics

So when the industrialist, business owner, service providers understand these methods why those are very important in the digital marketing field and the need of online presence for any business in current situation then this will become very easy to implement the online marketing strategies in their industry or field.

Digital Marketing job openings are everywhere around the world. Need to learn digital marketing courses thoroughly to perform well in the industry. When you complete the digital marketing training from the institute at Academy, your confidence level would be high and you can easily get the job as desired.

The Main Channels of Digital Marketing Courses

Websites

The online presence is very very important to any of the business for the present generation in the current marketing situation as without the website or information on online about your business which can't be taken far away. So that the websites which is having the complete details about your business and gives more information to your clients or consumers and makes them know more about your business and its functions. So without the online presence, it is hard to reach more people and create the awareness about the products and brand name.

Content Marketing

Why is content very important in digital Marketing field or online marketing? As the content is the king of all the other chapters of digital marketing or online marketing because when consumer visit a shop directly to purchase or in☐uire about any of the product in the shops the shopkeeper will explain them thoroughly the features and benefits of the products.

But when it comes to the online platform, the content itself will act/work as a sales executive or shopkeeper so here the content will be your representative on behalf of your business. So the content is going to bring more customer, visitors or business towards your website when you write a uni☐ue content on your webpage by itself the content starts speaking about your products and companies.

SEO/ Search Engine Optimization

This is one of the processes which allow you to list and run your websites online or search engines like (Google, Bing, Yahoo, Ask.com, AOL, Baidu, DuckDuckGo etc.) without making any payment to them. But the very important thing in this is it is not so easy to rank in SERP/ Search engine result page as there are several websites have already been listed under these search engine platforms so which needs to work hard to rank better in search engine result page. This process is called as a Search Engine Optimization.

Google Ads

Google ads are one of the very best tools to promote the products, services, or brands anywhere and everywhere across the world. The tool Google AdWords which is consists of multiple options in this software. Google Ads will provide an instant result for any campaigns. To create a better a campaign of your brand awareness and services the Google ads will provide a very good platform for the business owners, corporate sectors and the service providers around the world to reach their target audience through the Google AdWords channel. It is one of the main paid modules digital marketing courses.

SMM / Social Media Marketing

Social media marketing is one of the very effective methods in digital marketing strategies. The social media marketing tools are involved with various social media sites. The major SMM tools are (Facebook, Twitter, LinkedIn, Google+ YouTube, Pinterest, Instagram, etc.) these tools are very effective to reach the people around the world within a few seconds of time. By using or implementing the strategies of social media in any kind of services or business field is really going to give them the hundred percent results in their Social Media Marketing campaigns. SMM can be learned with digital marketing courses.

Email Marketing

Email marketing is one of the very old marketing methods and effective ways to send an individual newsletter and other subjects to the particular person by using the one's e-mail id. This form will exist even in future too, in spite of many others marketing channels, however, the e-mail marketing will be continued as earlier without any hamper. As an email marketing methods are completely different than the other marketing methods. It is also one of the main modules of Digital Marketing courses.

Mobile Marketing

The word mobile marketing sounds very familiar to each of us due to the people are very familiar and fond of with this device. Hence, this will be one of the most important factors of marketing with this tool. There is no limit for using of mobile phones and the device will be with the people at all the time. So the mobile marketing which targets the audience or users of active internet users and non-active internet users on their mobile phones. The difference between active internet users and non-active internet users when the user is using the smartphone with data on his device this can be considered as an active internet user.

Non-active is not connected with data or internet. There are multiple options to reach the non-active internet users by sending a text message, voice message and by calling directly to their contact number and letting them know about the features and services of the product. For active internet users, you can directly reach or send to their inbox (email), WhatsApp, Facebook, Twitter and other social media accounts as well. These kinds of marketing strategies are followed in mobile marketing. This module is also consisting of digital marketing courses.

To learn the entire processes of Digital Marketing Courses need to join a reputed digital marketing training institute. At the institute in Bangalore, we train the students from basics to advanced level marketing methods and strategies of online marketing. Which has to be followed thoroughly and this will help them to learn each step during their training with practical knowledge.

When you read all the above-mentioned information, you can easily understand that the importance of digital marketing and the trends of current online marketing situations also the advantages and benefits of its implementation in any of the industry, business or services around the world to promote and reach more of your targeted audience/Customers across the globe to get better results on the ROI (return on the investment). So the digital marketing industry is going to be the next hopes for better business results and career growth in coming years.